JAMES R BREWER

BUDGETING WITHOUT MONEY

A WORKBOOK TO CREATE A PERSONAL FINANCIAL PLAN BUILT AROUND YOUR LIFE GOALS

Platypus Publishing

First published by Platypus Publishing 2022

First edition

Cover design - Corrin Elizabeth Sheaffer

Find out more at brevityart.work

This book was professionally typeset on Reedsy.
Find out more at reedsy.com

If it were not for my family, this book would never have come about. They were the instigators; they are interwoven in the content; they will always be my inspiration.

Contents

IV HOW

V WHEN

Preface

This budgeting book was birthed by my family. You see, the members of my family write. My wife edits, ghostwrites, and publishes articles; this skill has been passed on to my kids. One has his MFA, another published a children's book, one writes poetry, one has written a novel, and one is exploring his talent in writing with his guitar. Then there is me. I write in birthday cards, which I give to my wife and kids. That's about it.

This past Father's Day, my wife gave me a gift. It was a class on how to write a book. At first, I wondered what I would do with this gift. I am not a writer. As I pondered this gift, I reviewed the various topics I personally would like to read. Then my wife suggested the obvious - budgeting. She tells me I am constantly discussing the various budgeting programs I have tried. She actually called it "complaining", but we will not go there. I have always kept a budget and even taught budgeting classes through a non-profit. I also handle the finances of my current employer. You could say I have been budgeting for 30-plus years.

This book is about my thoughts on budgeting. Within these pages are things I have learned and things I am currently walking through. Budgeting to me, is much more than numbers. It requires more thought than keeping track of income and expenses. Budgeting requires vision before determining what categories you need to manage. My goal in writing this book was to take a different approach to how we deal with our money.

You will find chapters discussing psychology, philosophy, accounting, and finances. Together we will explore what you want in life and how to use a budget to get there. You will read various stories to help you grasp the subject. Most of these stories are from my own life, but some are a combination of different stories that have been shared with me. The names are changed to protect their privacy, and the subject matter may be altered so you can understand the main point being communicated.

The goal of this book is to help you find purpose and learn to develop a practical budget that supports your vision. I appreciate you joining me in learning how to Budget Without Money.

I

WHERE

If you do not change direction, you may end up where you are heading.

Lao Tzu

1

Where To Start

For those ready to jump in, I created this first chapter to explain our road map. Most of what is here would have been in the introduction, but if you're like me, you tend to skip the introduction and start reading chapter 1. This is where we begin, and it is designed to prepare our mindset for where we are going with this book and where we will be when we finish.

A couple of years ago, Father's Day was coming up. My kids asked me what I wanted. I told them I wanted a gift I could treasure for the rest of my life. I wanted something that would also impact their lives. I then asked each one of them to write me a letter. The letter needed to include a list of things they wanted to do in their life. Basically, I wanted them to create a bucket list. One of the greatest gifts a parent can have is to see their kids develop a vision for their lives, to see their children dream, and to have a plan on how to reach that dream. A window into their purposes and aspirations was one of the best Father's Day presents I've ever received.

Do you have a bucket list? Do you know where your life is taking you?

Do you feel like someone hit the pause button in the last few years, and you finally found the remote so you can hit play again? No more floating around in life as things keep passing you by. It's time to take steps forward.

Let me be upfront: budgeting is not the answer, but it is a vital piece to help you build the life your desire. Budgets need small, disciplined steps that draw you closer to your goals. Progress can be small, but progress always comes one step at a time. When we do not see instant results, the temptation to quit can creep up on your doorstep and bring numerous distractions that offer an escape from the pressures and stresses of life. These may provide temporary relief but in the end only promise longer times of regret.

To overcome temptation, we need motivation, something that keeps us focused and strengthens our resolve to push through until we obtain our desired outcome. This is why this book was written, to help both you and I dig deep and find the things that will help us keep moving forward. We want to live without regret and enjoy the life we have been given.

The title, Budgeting Without Money, came about because I saw something was missing in my budgeting process. For years I budgeted my money as a good steward of my resources; making sure I never spent more than I earned. I even taught classes on how to manage personal finances. A budget was a means to be faithful with what I had. It was a process of ensuring I was in control of my spending. For most of my life, budgeting was a way to record history, what I earned and what I spent.

Budgeting is something that people tend to do when their finances are already a mess, or when they admit it is the responsible thing to do. They do this out of necessity even before evaluating where they want their life to go. We all know we need to manage our money, get control of our spending, and be responsible. However, budgeting can quickly become a record of what we have already done rather than a plan to take us where we want to go. We fail to do the hard work of discerning our life's direction and how budgeting can be a tool to help us realize our dreams. Budgeting works with money, but it should not start with money. A journey needs to be taken before we can deal with our finances. We need to budget without money before we can budget with money. This book is a part of that journey that will take you through the steps before money and how money should be used to take you on life's journey.

The process is laid out in four sections, five if you include this one. The first section is the WHY. This section is critical. Without it, this book becomes the same old budgeting book. This is the part where we budget without money. If we do not have a vision and a purpose, we tend to eventually stop doing the things that help us move forward in life. The second section is the WHAT. We will explore what a budget is, the various types of budgets, and some of the obstacles in budgeting. Section three is the HOW. This is where the rubber meets the road. We will walk through making a unique budget based on your personal why and how you have developed your vision while reading this book. The last section, I call WHEN. I call it WHEN because it made sense in following the WHERE, WHY, WHAT, and HOW. In this section, I describe when our budgets need flexibility, some last-minute pointers when your budget is struggling, and a brief analysis of a few different budgeting programs currently available on the internet.

* * *

Take a few minutes before you go to the next chapter and dream.

When you day dream, where does your mind wonder?

____

____

____

____

What are some of the things on your bucket list?

____

____

____

____

Let's get started with Budgeting Without Money!

II

WHY

We need to be fueled by vision, not by survival.

Travis Jones

2
Why Begin Here

In the original 1984 Karate Kid movie, there is a scene where Daniel is frustrated with the training he is receiving from Mr. Miyaki. After four days of work, Daniel feels more like a personal servant than a student. He has sanded the deck floor, waxed five cars, painted the fence, and painted Mr. Miyaki's house. Daniel, tired and frustrated, announces he is quitting. He felt he had learned nothing about karate. Mr. Miyagi asks Daniel to show each move associated with each task. Mr. Miyagi throws punches at Daniel, and with each punch, Daniel blocks them, using a move his body had learned from the continual repetition he performed with each task. Suddenly, his training now has a purpose connected to his why. That moment transformed his frustration into vision.

When I started to write this book, I wanted it to be more than just a method for managing your money. Budgeting has to be more than just doing an assignment. Dealing with our finances has to have an objective and vision behind it. We need to connect our task of being faithful with what we have to our purposes in life. To do this, we need to study ourselves and our behaviors and make adjustments so that our lives align with our vision of where we want to go.

Managing our money has just as much to do with psychology as it does math. It requires patience, vision, self-control, and the development of productive habits.

In the introduction of the book, The Psychology of Money, Morgan Housel says this...

"Doing well with money has little to do with how smart you are and a lot to do with how you behave. And behavior is challenging to teach, even to really smart people. A genius who loses control of their emotions can be a financial disaster. The opposite is also true; ordinary folks with no financial education can be wealthy if they have a handful of behavior skills that have nothing to do with formal measures of intelligence."[1]

Learning new behaviors require a change in how we think. The mind is our greatest asset and can also be our worse liability. Our thoughts determine our direction and view of life and affect our emotions. It can be based on truth or a lie.

Let me give you an example...

One night I led a meeting of a few families at my office, about three miles from home. My wife and kids joined me for the meeting which resulted in us having two cars at the office. After my wife left, I closed up the office and drove home. When I arrived at our house, my 9-year-old son was not there. I thought he went with my wife; she thought he went with me. Panic set in. I quickly drove back to the office, and when I got there, all of the lights were on. I had turned them all off when I left. The front door was wide open. I had locked everything up. The office was out in a wooded area, and my mind was racing with some bad possibilities.

---

1 Housel, Morgan. *The Psychology of Money*. Narrated by Chris Hill, Audible, 2020.

Where was my son?

We called the police. We called friends. We had people looking everywhere. Almost an hour was gone; still no answers. Statistics say that if your child is not found in the first hour, the chances of finding them drop dramatically. My mind told me he had been abducted, that he was lost forever.

Some time later, we received a phone call from the police. They found my son, or more specifically, he found them at a grocery store. Apparently, when I left the office, he was in the bathroom. Coming out into a dark office, he turned the lights on. Seeing me driving away in my car, he ran after me and, in a rush, forgot to close the door. After the first 100 yard dash, he started walking towards home, avoiding strangers, and looking for sites that were familiar to him. About two miles later he went into a grocery store where he saw a police officer and told him he was lost. The officer looked at my son and correctly guessed his name since he had heard the report of his missing. My son was brought home to us, and besides being a little tired from all the stress and running, he was fine. It was an emotional roller coaster.

My mind said he was lost, so my emotions followed. My mind went to worse-case scenarios when in reality, my son was smart enough to stay away from strangers and find someone he could trust. Our emotions follow our thoughts.

We have to begin with the process of our thinking, or we are doomed to repeat the same mistakes over and over again. Who said that insanity is doing the same thing over and over again and expecting different results? Oh yes, it was Albert Einstein. All would agree, he was pretty smart and accomplished a few things in his lifetime. So we do not keep repeating the same things over and over; we need to evaluate how we think, what we want in life, why we want it, and how to proceed forward to accomplish it. We do not begin with money. We start with the mind and the heart. These are our greatest assets. Stepping back and evaluating them will ensure that we are headed in the right direction and have the right tools for the journey.

The right mindset commits to the effort, time, and sacrifice required to manage a budget and produces a life of satisfaction and accomplishment.

I will say this several times in this book; budgeting is a tool. Learning how to use this tool will help steer you in the right direction and help you avoid many pitfalls. But before we budget with money, we need to budget with our why.

So, let's get to work and discover your WHY.

3

Why Discovered

So, you are reading a book on budgeting. Why? It could be because someone gave it to you as a gift. You know they will probably ask you about the book, so you had better read it. It could be that you want to develop a budget because it is the adult thing to do. That's a start. You may want to be responsible. You are moving in the right direction. You may see your that finances are in trouble, and you want to relieve your anxiety. That is also good. But before you can create a budget, it's important to find out why, and even more imperative to determine the goals you want the budget to help you reach.

A few years ago, I was listening to a Podcast by Dean Graziosi.[2] He asked his audience "Why do we do what we do?" Someone taught him the importance of digging deeper to find his true why. This was accomplished by asking himself why he does something. Then he asks why of his why seven more times. Each time coming closer to the root of his why.

---

2 Graziosi, Dean. *The Dean Graziosi Show*. 2019. Podcast. https://www.deangraziosi.com/podcast-episodes/

One morning I woke up early and as my normal routine dictates, I took my dog for a walk. It was dark outside, and the only ones awake were an old owl and the paper boy delivering the early addition. As I was walking, I asked myself why I was writing a book on budgeting.

My thoughts went something like this...

- I am writing this book because I want to get my thoughts down.
- I want to get my thoughts down because I want clarity.
- I want clarity because I want to know what is true.
- I want to know what is true so I can have confidence in the future.
- I want confidence in the future because I am afraid.
- I am afraid because I do not want to fail in providing for my family.
- I want to provide for my family because it is my responsibility.
- It is my responsibility because I love them, and I want to care for them.

Well, I went eight deep, but who is counting? I think you get the picture. Our why is what motivates us. It keeps us going. It is our goal, our prize, and what we fight for. Our why enables us to say no to some things and yes to other things. It is our compass that gives us direction and meaning. If we do not know our why, we just drift. When we drift into a state of uncertainty, fear and anxiety will rule us, and regret will be waiting around the corner to take advantage of us.

I heard another podcast featuring Simon Sinek, the author of the bestselling book Start With Why.[3] He suggested you ask a friend why they consider you as their friend. They will usually answer with the

---

3 Robbins, Tony. The Tony Robbins Podcast. Dec 10 2017.

same description of what makes a good friend: like how dependable you are, or that you both enjoy the same things. Go deeper. It can be hard to put into words, but the answer you are looking for is rooted in how you affect them. Eventually, they will stop talking about you and start talking about themselves and how you make them feel. They will tell you the purpose you serve in their life. They will be describing your why.

If we live without a why we live in ambiguity. Ambiguity breeds fear. Fear takes over because we live in the unknown and feel like we are wasting our lives. We tend to default to self-absorbed activities that distract us from reality. We end up living in our own little world and become self-centered, and self-centered people are the most miserable people I know.

We don't want to be miserable. In fact, not wanting to be miserable can be one of our chief motivators. Misery is pain on the inside. I was listening to a book by Nir Eyal called Indistractable.[4] In this book, he talks about motivation. He refers to a study on motivations that produce change, and the conclusion was that our desire to be relieved from pain motivates us. Specifically, the pain from wanting. When we want something, and we do not have it, we are motivated to do something. This want brings discomfort, and we do not like discomfort. It could be something as simple as thirst. We are thirsty. We want a drink of water, so we get out of our easy chair, go to the kitchen, and get a tall glass of cold refreshing water. Our want of thirst motivates us to move, to change, to do something to relieve this want.

What do you want? What pain are you trying to relieve? A budget can help only when you see a connection between keeping a budget and what

---

[4] Eyal, Nir. Indistractable, 2019. Audible, Inc

you want. You will no longer maintain the budget when that connection is broken. When this connection brakes, your bank account is soon to follow. A broken bank account is no fun. I would call that misery.

We tend to forget the connection between the desire and the process. Once our want is temporarily satisfied, we move on to fulfill another desire. We are constantly moving from one want to another. We now want to relax, so we lay down on the couch. We get a text from a friend about playing basketball, but we are resting. Then there is the battle between wanting relaxation and wanting to be with friends. Friends win out. There are more wants there. We like our friends and want to be with them. Exercise is good for us. We actually feel like we did something today; another want satisfied. The more wants you have on one side can motivate you to not fulfill the desires on the other side. Nir Eyal calls this stacking your wants. It is one way to increase motivation.

Why all this talk on motivations, wants, whys? It is because you want to change. That is why you are reading this book. We all desire to grow, to become a better person. It is a part of being human. We are made to learn, explore, create, and improve things. We invent, discover, accomplish, and take old things and make them new. When we do this, it brings joy, satisfaction, and a sense of well done. Is that not what we all long to hear at the end of our lives, "Well done."?

Can a budget do all of this for you? No. But it is a vital piece of the puzzle; without it, getting there becomes extremely hard. Every company has a budget. Every explorer refers to a map. Every inventor needs a plan so he can create. Money is essential, and managing it is crucial. A budget is a plan, a road map, a tool. The purpose of a budget is to help you fulfill your why.

So, what is your why? Deep down, what want do you desire to satisfy? Where do you want to be when you look at the end of your life? These are hard questions, and they take time to answer. Sometimes they are uncomfortable. Sometimes the answers are unnerving. The answers are what will produce real, sustainable change in your life.

Imagine yourself being a reporter, and you were given the assignment to find out how people view their lives. Most of what the young people talk about is what they will do. Most middle age people talk about where they are in life with a combination of how they accomplished it and where they are going. Most older people have their past dominate the conversation.

When we are closer to the end of our lives and our productivity is reduced, and we feel like our contribution is not what it used to be, we tend to realize our own mortality. We may look back and talk about some great memories, but regret always comes around.

Here is a summary of what people have said...

- They wish they had spent more time with family.
- They wish they had deeper friendships.
- They wish they had taken more risks.
- They wish they had followed their dreams.
- They wish they had taken better care of their lives.
- They wish their careers had a more significant impact on the community.
- They wish they had not worked so much.
- They wished they had been kinder to others.
- They wished they had enjoyed life more.
- They wished they had forgiven more.

Do you see a trend? Most of these have to do with relationships. Our lives become more fulfilling when we do what we do because we have relationships with others. Focusing on others involves stepping out, following dreams, and taking risks. These things take planning. It's time to stop drifting and start moving forward. It's time to live without regrets but do so with intention and purpose. It's time to discover your why.

Finding your why takes effort to dig deep. Keep asking yourself the hard questions. I will give you a little hint. For most people, they find fulfillment in positively affecting others. Our dreams may be reaching for the sky, but our roots run deep in the lives of others.

You can start simply by taking time and writing down the answers to a few questions. As you have time, move deeper into why you do the things you do. Finally, you will dig into the why that drives your life. This will take some uninterrupted thought time. So put away all distractions, force yourself to take the next step, and discover your why.

* * *

Here are a few questions to get your started...

When do you feel purpose in your life?

____

____

____

____

What regrets do you fear?

At the end of your life, what do you desire people to say about you?

Why are you working on a budget? Ask why of your why seven times.

1.
2.
3.
4.
5.
6.
7.

4
Measuring Your Values

My hobby is woodworking. Taking raw wood, cutting it, sanding it, putting pieces together, and staining it; then sitting back and seeing my creation. It can be satisfying when you see the end results, and it can also be frustrating when you make mistakes in the process. One tool I use is a tape measure. The tape measure tells me where to make my cuts so my pieces fit together correctly. There is a saying, "Measure twice, cut once." I can't tell you how often I cut in the wrong spot because I only measured once.

One of the tools for measuring if your life is heading in the right direction is your values. Your values are the things that have meaning for you. They are your definable goals for how you live your life. Values measure your life to see if it is turning out as you hoped it would. As you measure your life by your values, you stay on track.

You have values, even if you do not know what they are. There are times you feel great and times you feel regretful. These emotions are pointers showing you what your values are. They are revealing what is important to you.

Your why is your deep-rooted motivator and keeps you pressing forward when things get tough. It is the heart behind all you do. Your values are expressions of your why, like how your bones give your body definition.

When I speak of values regarding budgeting, I am not necessarily talking about the importance of honesty or dependability. These values speak more about who you are as a person. Values in budgeting is more about the life you want to live, the things that make you happy, give meaning and purpose, and make you proud as you look back on your life. Money then becomes a means to help support your values. Values give you the WHAT in managing your money.

My wife and I like to take walks together. Our dog Emmy usually joins us and makes sure we stay on pace. She walks faster than us and keeps us moving, especially if there is a squirrel, deer, chipmunk, dog, or just another person she wants to meet. We talk when we walk, and the conversation regularly focuses on our values, the things we enjoy and that are worth our time. We are looking ahead in life and asking ourselves what we want life to be like in ten years. We tend to focus on three values. The first is being generous. We want to be generous with our time, our money, and our abilities. We want to be generous to our kids, our church, and those around us who are less fortunate. We also talk about being active. We like walking, biking, hiking, and traveling. As we get older, we want to be healthy enough to do these things. Time with our family is also a great value to us. If you think about it, we have fully invested more of ourselves, our time, energy, and money into our kids than anything else in our lives. We love our kids and help them in any way we can. We enjoy being around them. We love making moments with them. My wife is big on making moments. We want to be able to visit them wherever they live, go on vacations with them, and be a part of their lives. This is valuable to us.

When your life lines up with your values, you feel good. You are satisfied and generally happy. When your life and values do not line up, you feel discontent, irritable, and basically unhappy.

Values help you make the right decisions. Do you take that job, make that purchase, even marry that person? Understanding your values brings balance to your life. It makes decision-making easier. It helps reduce complexity and minimize confusion. Values address the questions on what we should do. When values anchor our choices, we can make confident decisions.

Like cutting we need to constantly measure twice when we make decisions, or our life will repeatedly go off course. There are many distractions in life that want to redirect us. Our values keep us heading in the right direction, so we get what is best rather than settling for what is good.

Prioritizing your values is also essential because, at different times, they can conflict with each other. My wife and I have five children, so managing birthdays and budgets can be difficult. When our kids were younger, we celebrated their birthdays, but each birthday would not be celebrated in the same way. On even birthdays, they could invite several friends, but on odd year birthdays, they could only invite one friend. We had the value of wanting to bless our kids with something big and help them connect with all their friends. We also had the value of not spoiling them and teaching them to manage the family resources, so we could not always afford the big party. Alternating how we celebrated birthdays helped us communicate these values to our kids.

A common conflict is the value of socializing with friends and the importance of living within your means. Your friends always want to eat out, but your budget can not always afford this extra expense. Values need to be managed and prioritized. You can also come up with less expensive ideas like games nights and pot-luck dinners.

Once you have a list of core values you want in your life, you need muscles to help these values move. Our muscles are used to move us forward. They propel us in a direction. The muscles that are attached to the bones of our values are called activities. Activities are things you do that display your values. It is taking your values and breaking them down into measurable actions.

I said one of my values was being active, so I take walks daily. I also bike several times a week. How we eat also applies to this. My wife tries to provide healthier meals. It doesn't help when I bring home pizza. Perhaps I have not fully embraced the healthy eating principle.

Eating healthy does affect the budget. Healthy foods tend to cost more, so meals need to be planned better. We do more smoothies rather than ice cream. I recently found out how much sugar is in a smoothie you buy at a smoothie shop. Yikes! Now we make our own at home. This past year we have gone through two Magic Bullets (blender).

Values, with your activities, help you make the right decisions. You now have a purpose and a reason you do what you do. No longer are you stressed about what decision you should make. If it does not align with where you are going in life and your values, then you say no. You are focused on the prize. Not only does this affect budgeting, but this will help you with career decisions, with your free time management, and even with whom you will spend your life with. Values reflect who you are and who you want to be.

That is enough about me and my illustrations. What about you? Take some time, and think about your life. Where are you, what makes you happy, what do you enjoy? By the way, this is a process, and things can change over time. This is a part of being human. Enjoy the ride, don't stress about it but be active in choosing where you want your life to go. Stress comes from not knowing; procrastination breeds regret; stop asking yourself why you did not start sooner and begin the process now. Moving forward and not standing still is one way to bring peace and enjoyment to life. Why not take the next step now?

* * *

List 3 values you want in your life and two activities for each value.

Value 1: ______________________________

1. ______________________________
2. ______________________________

Value 2: ______________________________

1. ______________________________
2. ______________________________

Value 3: ______________________________

1. ______________________________
2. ______________________________

5
Habits Are Hobbits

Habits are like Hobbits. Even if you have not seen The Lord of the Rings movies or read the books, you probably know what a Hobbit is. For those who do not know, they are little people who mind their own business and live their lives the same way year after year. For Middle Earth, most would have called them insignificant. In the same way, habits are small things, being repeated over and over, and in themselves don't seem to make a significant impact. A Hobbit could easily be overlooked. But it was the Hobbit who turned everything around and saved Middle Earth. Habits will do the same for you. The small, consistent things building up over time can have the most significant impact on your life.

We are creatures of habit; we wake up about the same time; we eat meals around the same time; we drive the same route to work every day. Habits can be good, like the writer who daily makes himself sit down to write for two hours even though he does not feel inspired. It can help us stay healthy by building a workout schedule. We are most productive when we have a routine, which is another way of saying a habit. Habits can also not be good, like eating Chocolate Mousse Tracks ice cream every night or playing video games on our phones all day.

I am talking about habits in a budgeting book because your budget is a reflection of your spending habits. Some habits can be good, like scheduling when to pay your bills, and others can be bad, like eating out for lunch every day when you cannot afford it. The worst habit of all when it comes to money is avoidance. It is easier to binge on Netflix than do what we know we should do. We all feel the stress of life, especially when we look at our bank account, wondering who robbed us of our hard-earned money. When we do not know what to do, we move on to something less stressful. When we avoid managing our money, we just add fuel to the fire. Things will only get worse. Moving on to distractions may give us temporary relief from our stressful life, but they do not address the problem. Instead, the weight of our problem just grows.

In his book Atomic Habits, James Clear lays out the four steps of a habit.[5] They are cue, craving, reaction, and reward. It works like this. We just had an argument with our spouse (friend, parent,..) and we feel stressed out. This is the cue. As a result, we crave relief and react by grabbing our laptops, flopping down on the couch, and scrolling through social media to distract us from the stressful situation. This temporary distraction is enough to remove the stress; thus, we have our reward. But the problem never goes away. Even though we all need downtime, this habit of avoidance is not a good habit to default to.

So how do we develop good habits? It starts with planning. We do this before we are in the heat of a situation. If we take some time to think through our lives, we will see patterns in how we deal with problems. One way to bring clarity, is to pretend that it is someone else' problem and they are asking your advice. What would you recommend they do? Another thing we can do is to talk to someone we respect, asking for

---

[5] Clear, James. Atomic Habits, 2018. Penguin Audio.

their advice. When we plan and act, old habits can be broken, and new habits that can positively affect us can be established.

It is vital to take some time to write out our problems, those things we tend to avoid. Use James Clear's four steps of developing a habit to break old habits and cultivate new ones.

- What issue causes the stress (the cue)?
- Now, what do we desire (craving)? Dig deep and define it.
- How do you usually respond (reaction)? Now ask yourself what your response should be? Find a preferable alternative that will produce a better and more productive outcome.
- Lastly, treat yourself to something special (reward).

Moving one step at a time is progress. Simple, easy steps of progress are fulfilling. For an example, let's create a habit of dealing with your bills instead of stressing out when you get them, forgetting where you put them, and then freaking out when you get a late notice. You can create a place for your bills. It could be a drawer, a particular spot on your desk, or on a table in the corner of your bedroom; you get the idea.

The next thing is creating a cue to remind you to take care of them. Set a reminder on your phone, say 9:00 on Saturday mornings. You can also set up another cue, like not getting your morning coffee until all your bills are laid out and ready for you to review.

I would also suggest removing all distractions. As you look at your bills, you may be tempted to escape by grabbing your phone to text a friend, check the weather, or even play a game. Put the phone in another room.

Set a goal like planning when each bill is due and when you will pay it. Laying out a goal of what you want to accomplish helps you move forward. Organizing your bills once a week does bring clarity and aids in relieving stress since ambiguity is stressful in and of itself. You now know what you owe, when it is due, and if you have the money to cover it. I know not having enough money to cover bills is stressful. We will get to this later in the book.

You need to reward yourself for taking this first step. It could be playing your video game for a few minutes, going for a walk, or even treating yourself to a piece of chocolate. Something simple that you enjoy, just don't spend a lot of money on it.

When I played various sports as a teen, we all dreaded the conditioning aspect of practice. Running multiple sprints was exhausting. To help us overcome this dreadful experience, we would psych ourselves up and make it a competition. This motivated us to push ourselves and distract us from the pain of fatigue. It even added a little enjoyment to the process.

Unless you are a budget nerd, excitement is probably not your first reaction when organizing your finances. For most of us, budgeting is viewed as tedious and limiting. The goal is to turn something dreadful into something enjoyable. We need to re-imagine budgeting as a challenge waiting to be conquered. When something is fun, it helps us keep our focus. When we have a challenge, there is excitement when we win. The battle is all in our minds. Change how you think, and you will change your outcome.

You can also add some creativity to your budget. Not with the numbers but with the categories. You can name them whatever you want. If you use a spreadsheet, you can add color. When you see your budget as a game or a puzzle that you can win, you tend to put more focus and effort into it. You have a creative side, so use it to your advantage.

Here are some interesting statistics on habits...

1. About 40% of your activities are automatic behaviors
2. Habits save you time and energy
3. It usually takes 66 days to change a habit
4. Habits reflect your past goals[6]

Here is a power thought by Stephen Covey, "Sow a thought, reap an action; sow an action, reap a habit; sow a habit, reap a character; sow a character, reap a destiny."[7]

Your habits are your building blocks that create the house where your vision lives. Without habits, your dreams are left out in the cold. Forming the right habits empowers you to say yes to the things that support your values and no to the temptations that drain your resources. Put away distractions, form new habits, and the results will be realized with your consistent effort over time.

As you think about your habits, just remember what the hobbit Bilbo Baggins said, "Go back? No good at all! Go sideways? Impossible! Go forward? Only thing to do! On we go![8]

* * *

---

[6] https://medium.com/@susannekrausedx/5-interesting-facts-about-habits-76fffa6f291f

[7] Covey, Stephen. The 7 Habits of Highly Effective People: Powerful Lessons in Personal Change, 2004, Simon & Schuster Audio Tolkien,J.R.R. 2012 The Hobbit. London

[8] Tolkien,J.R.R. 2012 The Hobbit. London, England: Harpper Collins

Look back at your values and activities. Now, name a few habits needed to make these activities a reality.

Habit 1:

____

What is my cue: ______________________________

What am I craving: ____________________________

How should I react: ___________________________

What is my reward: ___________________________

Habit 2:

____

What is my cue: ______________________________

What am I craving: ____________________________

How should I react: ___________________________

What is my reward: ___________________________

Habit 3:

____

What is my cue: ______________________________

What am I craving: ____________________________

How should I react: ___________________________

What is my reward: ___________________________

6

Spoken Thoughts

An old proverb says, "As a man thinks, so is he."[9] Your thoughts shape who you are. In the book Rich Dad, Poor Dad by Robert Kiyosaki, the author describes the mindset of two father figures in his life.[10] Both were educated, had good-paying jobs, and worked hard at what they did. They were honest, good men who cared for Robert and wanted him to succeed. But each man viewed life differently. Robert begins the book with a statement that reveals the mindset of each dad when they encounter a question about a purchase. The poor dad says, "We cannot afford it," and the rich dad says, "How can we afford it?" One is a statement that ends the conversation. The other challenges the mind to explore options, create paths to success, and looks for ways to overcome obstacles. How our mind views life will determine what we do next.

Have you ever thought about what you think? Your mind is a powerful tool that shapes your life. It affects how you feel, which affects your motivation, which affects your body. Your thoughts can

---

9 Proverbs 23:7

10 Kiyosaki, Robert. Rich Dad Poor Dad, 2017, Brilliance Audio

paralyze you or propel you into action. If you think you are a failure, then you feel like a failure, and then you act like a failure, reinforcing your belief that you are a failure. It is a vicious cycle.

When you believe something about yourself, your attention is drawn toward that belief. Your mind is subconsciously looking for evidence that your view about yourself is accurate. Evidence that leans in this direction is now called fact, and evidence that opposes it is called chance. How you think determines how you interpret what happens in your life.

Let's say you have a job interview. You do not feel ready, and you have thoughts that you are not good enough. You enter the waiting area, and you see three other candidates. One is dressed really sharp; you wonder why you picked the outfit you wore. The next one has a nice leather portfolio with a Mont Blanc pen. You realize you have no paper or pen to take notes; you feel unprepared. The following person looks relaxed and is as calm as a cucumber; you are a nervous wreck. Your feelings of inadequacy are now screaming at you. Do you feel confident when it is your opportunity to go into the interview? Are you at your best?Probably not. If you do not think and feel your best, then you will not present your best to the interviewer. Your beliefs affected your feelings which affected your performance, which affected the interview, and you end up not getting the job. This is what we call a self-fulfilling prophecy.

Henry Ford said it best, "Whether you think you can or think you can't, you are right."[11]

---

[11] https://quoteinvestigator.com/2015/02/03/you-can/#:~:text=The%20full%20adage%20evolved%20and,version%20ascribed%20to%20Henry%20Ford.

Thinking positively in and of itself does not change things, but what it can do is empower you to change your actions. Instead of obstacles and roadblocks, you see opportunities and challenges you can overcome. You are motivated to change, and your mind is no longer passive and defeated; it is active and finding ways to move forward. Positive thinking is a motivator.

You can change how you think. The first step is being aware of your focus. You are human, have flaws, and make mistakes in your life. Admit it, and now get over it. Don't take yourself so seriously. Confident people are not the ones who do not make mistakes, but they are the ones who do not let their errors define them. They brush them off and move on. Their faults do not make them think less of themselves; they just think of themselves less. Their focus is on what they are doing, who they are with, and what they are trying to accomplish. They realize they have not obtained perfection. They are learning, growing, and enjoying the process as they go through life.

What you need to do is to you to give yourself a little grace. We tend to beat ourselves up, preventing ourselves from trying again. Just remember Thomas Edison. He had over 1000 failures with his experiment on the lightbulb before he was successful. When asked about his failures, he said he did not fail. His lightbulb was invented with a 1000-step process.[12] He stayed focused on what he wanted to accomplish, and he did it.

Like the serenity prayer of Reinhold Niebuhr, we need to focus on the things we can change, not on the things we cannot control. Stress comes

---

[12] https://medium.com/cry-mag/thomas-edisons-theorem-for-success-b96591bf7dd1#:~:text=In%20the%201920s%2C%20a%20journalist,invented%20the%20first%20electric%20lamp.

from trying to change something we are not responsible for, like how people respond to us. We can influence their response, but we cannot control it. As a kid, I used to tell my parents that my older brother made me do it or that he made me mad. This was blame shifting. People's words and actions do affect you but they do not have to control you. No one determines how you think or how you respond. You do. You can take control of your thoughts and, thus, your actions. You have a choice.

Thinking correctly is the first step, but what we speak is also just as important. Another famous proverb goes something like this, "Life and death are in the power of the tongue; those who love it will eat its fruit."[13] Your words can bring encouragement or discouragement. We all know that words others say to us affect us. If someone is always talking down to us, we feel discouraged. We feel encouraged when an employer tells us what a great job we did. If other's words affect us, how much more do our own words?

Your words not only reflect what you believe, but they also reinforce what you believe. When our children were young, we would not only tell them what we expected them to do, we had them repeat out loud what we told them. When they repeated it, they took ownership of it and were more likely to remember it, and more likely to do it. Your words strengthen your beliefs.

If you can control your tongue, then you will direct your life. Some liken the tongue to a rudder of a boat that turns the boat where the captain wishes it to go.[14] When you speak out loud, you remind yourself of who you are and what your purpose is. Your words direct your focus and

---

[13] Proverbs 18:21

[14] James 3:4

strengthen you to keep moving forward, forgetting the failures of the past and pressing on to accomplish what you desire to achieve.

Your words can reinforce your goals and make them more real, or they can tear them down, so they no longer seem attainable. You do have a choice. You have the ability to change your life and your circumstances. The worst thing to do when you are not satisfied with life is to do the same thing over and over again. Remember the definition of "insanity?" Think about where you want to go. Stop listening to yourself (negative thoughts) and start speaking to yourself (positive reinforcement). Speak to yourself because you are worth it, and your life is worth living well. Every thought matters, and every word is impacts your life.

* * *

Take out a sheet of paper and...

1. Write down a goal you have or something you have been wanting to accomplish but have failed to act upon it.
2. On one side of the page list all you fears, anxieties and negative thoughts associated with failing. Include the failure of doing nothing.
3. On the other side of the paper, write down all the things that will happen if this goal is fulfilled. With every failure, counter it with a success in reaching your goal.
4. List all the small steps it will take to obtain this goal and share that plan with a friend, mentor, or significant other. Accountability helps propel us forward.
5. Everyday, look at the next step in the plan, and speak out loud words that affirm your ability to accomplish this one task. When you think a negative thought, counter it with a positive thought.
6. As these small tasks are completed, check them off. You will see your confidence grow as you move closer to reaching your goal.
7. Give yourself grace. None of us win all of the battles, but if we persevere we will win the war. Forget what lies behind and press forward to what is ahead of you. [15]

[15] Philippians 3:13

7

Environmentally Friendly

My son likes to watch reruns of a program called *Psych*. The story is about a guy who has developed excellent observation skills, which he uses to make others think he has psychic abilities. In one episode, they try to help the police solve a mystery involving a possible alien visitation. They need an alien expert, so they track down an old high school friend who was the sci-fi geek of the school. When they see him now, he acts like a sports jock, a complete turn-around of who he was in high school. This transformation was the result of peer pressure he received from his new friends and his very attractive wife. But inside, he was still a sci-fi geek. He even had a secret room with all his sci-fi paraphernalia. In the end, his wife finds the secret room, and he is exposed. Living two lives is no longer an option. As these stories typically go, his wife was also a closet sci-fi geek, so they lived happily ever after, or at least till the end of the show.

Peer pressure is real. Our brains are constantly receiving feedback from those around us. Inside we want to be accepted and even admired. Studies have shown that much of our self-worth and outlook on life is due to our social environment. We care what others think of us.

Whether you like to admit it or not, you are influenced by those you spend the most time with. If your friends smoke, your chances of being a smoker are high. If your friends care about the environment, you will likely share this value. If your friends are into working out and staying active, you are more likely to be an active person as well. It just makes sense; part of the reason you associate with them is that you like the same things and respect each other's values.

Have you ever noticed that when one person in a group is complaining about something in life, the rest of the group also tends to develop an attitude? They either complain about the topic or complain about the person complaining. Have you ever gone into a place and were greeted by a person with a warm, caring smile? You could tell this person loves life and loves people. You felt accepted, and you face smiles in response. Emotions are contagious. Positive people influence you to be positive. Negative people can shift you towards looking at life negatively. Our emotions absorb the emotions of our environment.

If you want to learn a new skill or grow in a particular area of your life, then associate with people that are good in that area. Find clubs, classes, and programs to help you develop new skills and expand your life experience. If you find that you are doing the same things and never growing, just look at the people you are around. Change your environment, and you will change your perspective.

What does this have to do with budgeting? Look at your spending patterns. Now, look at your friends' spending patterns. Are you all eating out a lot? Do you all depend on credit cards to survive?

As Darren Hardy writes in The Compound Effect:

"According to research by social psychologist Dr. David McClelland of

Harvard, [the people you habitually associate with] determine as much as 95 percent of your success or failure in life."[16]

That is a big impact on your life. It makes you want to evaluate with whom and where you spend your time.

I am not telling you to dump all your current relationships and move to another city. I am telling you to evaluate where you are and where you want to go. If you wish to change your life, you will need to make adjustments to your environment. You need places that encourage you to move forward, reinforce the values you want to embrace, and remind you of your goals in life.

Find clubs, support groups, and chat rooms representing the life you desire to experience. Expand your vision by expanding your experience. Take classes that help you grow and learn. Listen to a podcast on a subject you might be interested in. Pick up new habits and routines that bring interest and enjoyment to your soul. Love to learn, and you will learn to love life.

The idea is to position yourself for success. When you grow, your why is reinforced, and you are more motivated to use your budget to support your values. You are now more likely to work out those activities that enhance your life. Once you have a vision and are in the right environment, the probability of success is exceptionally high. Your mindset has changed, and now you are ready to make practical changes to your life.

* * *

[16] Hardy, David. The Compound Effect, 2019, Folio Literary Management

Think in relation to your values, activities, and finances:

Describe where do you want to be in one year?

____

Describe where do you want to be in five years?

List clubs, Facebook groups, classes, podcasts, or friends that would help me reach those goal?

8

Connecting With WHY

So, what does all this have to do with money and budgeting? Budgeting can be a challenging and tedious process. It is easy to get bogged down in the numbers and all the bills and forget the reason behind it all. We must continually remind ourselves of our why. Our why is described by our values. These values are lived out in our activities. Our finances make these activities a reality. Budgeting our finances is the plan that creates the future we want to live.

Change happens in our lives when we are motivated to no longer be the person we were. It happens when we are not satisfied with where we are in life. We create a picture of where we want to go, so we start developing a plan on how to get there. We are looking for that preferable future.

Creating reminders of your why and your values is your first step. You can put pictures on the refrigerator, beside your bed, and on the bathroom mirror. Tell yourself every time you see those pictures; "This is why I do what I do." When your values lead you to have practical goals, like getting out of debt or buying a house, having notes or numbers in key locations helps you stay focused on your dream.

The next step towards change is showing up. When we want to get in shape, we set the alarm and get out of bed when it goes off. Even though our bodies cry out for more sleep, we have already decided we want to change, so we go to the gym. When we keep our word to ourselves and workout, we feel so much better. Maybe a little physically sore, but inside we have the satisfaction of accomplishing something. We fought off the temptation to stay in bed and we showed up.

Your finances also need to get in shape. Just like working out, you need to take time to plan, and make sacrifices. It may even mean getting a part-time job or studying those at work who are successful and copying them. Showing up daily with a mindset that wants to learn and grow will take you places. A learning and growing life makes a happier person, and moves you bit by bit closer to your goal.

Part of showing up is also stepping out. Taking risks involves discomfort. Remember the phrase, "No pain; no gain." It is time to take a chance instead of gravitating to what we know and what feels comfortable. As you reflect on this, you will see the pain of taking a chance is far less than the pain of regret, misery, and fear that comes with doing nothing.

I am very conservative, and risk is not in my nature. Several years ago, I worked for a company that was bought out, which caused a restructuring within our region. My job was being eliminated. Everyone was either given a severance package or a job offer at the new location a few hundred miles away. I heard through the grapevine that I was being offered the job, not the severance package. I had about a week before the new VP arrived to meet with us. What would I do?

On one side: Our family was here; our friends were here; we were very involved in our church and community. We liked where we lived. But I needed a job to care for my family and pay for the mortgage. Currently, I had no substantial job offers in my area.

On the other side: The salary they were offering was excellent, and the new location was in a growing area. They would even pay for my family to move. It was a more secure option. I could care for my wife and kids. But, we would have to leave all of our friends and family.

The following week, I was called into the new regional vice president's office. He opened my packet and looked confused. I was being offered both options. They wanted me to stay with the company, so they offered me a new position, and yet they offered me a severance package as well. He thought HR messed up, but he had to present it since it was in my packet. I asked for the weekend to think about it.

To give you more insight on what possible other options were transpir-ing; a friend had started a business and asked for my help. The work amounted to a part-time job that paid about a quarter of my present salary. It could grow into full time, but it may take a year or two before this would happen.

My current employer's transition was not going smoothly and my position with the company gave me some specific insight into how things worked in our area. I began to wonder if I could do some consulting for them, at least for a couple of months. This would enable me to have time to find a higher paying job, or see if my friend's business was headed in the right direction financially.

My wife and I discussed the possibilities and sought counsel from trusted friends.

The weekend ended. I met with the VP. I decided to take the choice with the greater risk. I turned down the job offer and took the severance package. They asked me to stay on for another month, and I agreed to help.

After a couple of weeks, I went to my current boss and gave him a proposal to do contract work for them. All I asked for was a two-month contract. They accepted the agreement but would not guarantee any time frame. They thought it would be less than a month. Well, the contract lasted two years, and I was the one who ended it.

My friend's business grew, and he ended up hiring many more employees. Over those two years, I made more money than I ever had in my life. Initially, it was a risk and uncomfortable, but it was well worth it.

Risks are risky, but risks make life engaging and produce personal growth. We can minimize risk by researching, asking for advice, and studying others who have gone before us. When you take a chance, your values become more solidified, and your tolerance to change will expand. When we become a student of life, things become more interesting, and life becomes more enjoyable.

One more step towards change is eliminating your excuses. We tend to gravitate towards why we cannot do something instead of finding out how to get it done. Catch yourself when you give an excuse and ask yourself how to overcome it. This will take a lot of practice, but your thinking patterns will change as you focus on the thoughts that direct you to your next step.

* * *

Below is a summary of of where we are in our journey with budgeting without money:

1. Defining your why (CH 3)
2. Solidifying your values (CH 4)
3. Creating activities (CH 4)
4. Ways to support Your Goals:
    - Form right habits (CH 5)
    - Take captive your thoughts (CH 6)
    - Catch your words (CH 6)
    - Put yourself in the right environment (CH 7)
    - Posting reminders (CH 8)
    - Showing up (CH 8)
    - Step out of your comfort zone (CH 8)
    - Eliminating excuses (CH 8)

These steps will produce momentum propelling you forward in your life. As the Lexus car commercial says, "Don't dream it, drive it."

What fear have I not addressed that has prevented me from doing the previous chapters assignments? What will move me past this fear?

____

____

____

____

III

WHAT

It's clearly a budget. It's got a lot of numbers in it.

George W. Bush

9

What? A Budget?

One summer, my youngest daughter took a class on orienteering. For those who do not know what this is, it is a sport where you hike through the woods, trying to find checkpoints with a paper map and a compass. A state park near our house has an orienteering course, so our family went with our daughter to see what she had learned. When we reached one checkpoint, we needed a plan to find the next one. With the help of her compass, she had an idea of where she wanted to go, but too many obstacles were present to make a straight line towards it. The map showed a path near us that went in the same general direction. We followed my daughter's plan and moved forward. Walking the trail for part of the time helped, but we needed to trounce through the woods, cross over a stream, and climb over several fallen trees. Using her compass, my daughter weaved her way through the woods and spotted her destination. Her plan worked, and we arrived victorious at the next checkpoint.

You have a vision, a direction, a purpose in life. Like our orienteering expedition, you need a map and a plan to bring you there. You are not meant to drift through life, letting whatever comes your way run you over. You are designed to create, build, and overcome obstacles. Life requires participation, and the more you put into it, the more you will get out of it. A budget is a way that shows you are participating in life. You can do this. Progress takes one step at a time.

Let's face it; money is a big part of life. You need it to eat, provide shelter, buy clothes, and travel from one place to another. The majority of your life is spent earning money so you can do things you need to do and the things you enjoy doing. For most of us, money represents time. In high school, I worked for Mr. Moe's Subs. They did not pay me for the number of subs I made or how many square feet I cleaned. They paid me an hourly wage. I think I got $3.35 an hour. Yes, this was a few years ago. An hour of my time equaled $3.35 in cold, hard cash. This was not much, but it paid for gas in my car, eating out with my friends, and maybe even a movie with my date.

What is your time worth? Time is what you give to your employer, and you earn a paycheck in return. You trade your time for his money. So, what are you going to do with all your money? It's time to plan. If you do not, chances are you may waste it all. The plan for your money is called a budget. A budget gives you a clear idea of where your money came from and where it is going. Your money has a purpose now, making the rest of your time count for something.

When most people hear the word budget, they think of constraints, limits, the mean taskmaster telling them what to do or, more commonly, what not to do. They perceive the budget as a prison holding them back from enjoying life. A budget can be that if you possess no vision of what you want in life. But when you realize what you want, a budget becomes your compass to help direct you in obtaining your goals.

A budget is a road map. It is the GPS on your phone telling you when to turn, the various routes you can take, and the quickest way to arrive at your destination. It can be like the App Waze telling you the accidents and speed traps to avoid. Without a budget, we have a higher probability of getting lost. Once lost, we sit down in frustration, wondering where we have been and where we are now.

Like an explorers map or a builders blueprints, a budget is a tool that shows you the big picture and yet reveals to you the small details.

A budget is not a teleporter where you say, "Beam me up Scottie" and you magically arrive at your destination. Most people do not use the word effortless to describe budgeting. Sacrifice is required. But sacrifice is only giving up one thing so you can obtain something better.

A budget keeps you focused on your goals and prevents you from falling into the trap of spontaneous spending and impulse buying.

A budget takes away the ambiguity and provides purpose for every dollar. It gives a reason to all the time you spent earning that money. A budget is a plan for success.

As they say, if you fail to plan, you plan to fail. If you did not catch the thought, read that sentence again.

I do not want you to feel the regret of lost time, like I've felt too often in the past. I do not want you to wonder what happened to all that money you earned and if the time you spent working for it was wasted on things that take you nowhere. There is no sense of satisfaction when you wander in the fog of regret. A budget clears the fog and reduces your chances of regret.

Plans don't usually happen overnight. It takes time to develop and time to execute. It takes strategy, patience, and commitment. Obstacles and temptations will come, but the diligent will win the prize.

Let's shift gears and look at budgeting another way. My wife knows that I cannot teach anything without throwing in something about football. So, here is my football analogy...

I am not a New England Patriots fan nor a Tampa Bay Buccaneer enthusiast. However, Tom Brady, the GOAT of football, is to be admired.[17] At 45, he is still playing the game at a high level. He is known for his intense preparation, extreme diet, and unusual fitness routine. He came into the league as a sixth-round draft pick and still sees himself as an underdog. He makes sacrifices, like not taking the "big money" he deserves. He knows how to control his emotions and adjusts his strategies when the defense changes. He is continually learning, setting new goals, and aspiring to get better. His success is made one decision at a time. To him, a sacrifice is not a sacrifice as long as he moves one step closer to his goal. That is what a budget does. It takes you one step closer to your goal. Each step taken reveals your commitment and brings you closer to your desired objective.

Like Tom Brady adjusts as the defense changes, you too must be patient and adapt with the circumstances. To not change is complacency, and avoidance will only delay the inevitable. The end will be worse as we procrastinate. We build character as we deal with our problems, delay gratification, and gain control of our emotions. And possessing strong character allows us to make the right choices and have peace with

---

[17] https://www.thecoldwire.com/why-is-tom-brady-called-the-goat/#:~:text=Tom%20Brady%20is%20called%20the,him%20such%20a%20high%20distinction.

purpose in our decisions.

The purpose of a budget is to help us see on paper how we are doing with handling our problems. It gives us insight and helps bring clarity to our issues. A budget can bring hope as we find creative ways to map it out, so we can trounce through the forest of compromise, live up to the path of our obligations, and move closer to the flags of our goals. Just like my daughter did in the woods of her orienteering class.

* * *

Now it is your turn. What will a budget do for you?

____

____

____

____

____

10

Do You Like Options?

Whenever I use my GPS to give me directions to my destination, it usually provides me with several options. One option may be faster; one option may be a shorter distance; and one option may be more scenic. They all take me where I want to go; just the route is different.

Like the various directions on my GPS, there are different budgeting philosophies to help you plan out your finances. Ultimately, they all do the same thing by helping direct you to where you want to go. None of the options are wrong; it's a matter of perspective. Each style has its own merits, and each can also bring its pitfalls. Personal preference is the real difference because each one of us is unique. We each possess different learning styles, viewpoints, and ways in which we get things done. The important thing is that we are doing something and learning to manage our money. For this section, I hope to give a concise yet descriptive picture of each philosophy where you can identify what works best for you. In the end, a combination of a couple of these will probably be a good fit.

ZERO-BASED BUDGETING

One of the most popular is called zero-based budgeting. This philosophy is rooted in the idea that every incoming dollar is assigned to every outgoing expense. In the end, you have zero dollars left over. It allocates all funds based on current and anticipated needs rather than historical costs. Every category starts at $0.00 and you must justify why money is allocated to that need. Each month can look different depending on things anticipated for the particular month. In one sense, this is how we live. Christmas only comes once a year. Car insurance may only come every six months. Vacations do not happen every month, even though that would be nice. Zero-based budgeting does not mean we do not plan for those things; it means we allocate every dollar to a specific purpose. As the popular program called *You Need A Budget* (YNAB) says, every dollar has a job. When you get paid, all the money is allocated somewhere. Money does not just sit in the bank. The entirety of your money has a purpose.

The advantages of zero-based budgeting include flexibility, purposeful spending, and typically lower cost. It is flexible since every month's budget can look different. Let's say you bought a new car, so your budget for car repairs is significantly reduced, or maybe you are planning a big vacation overseas next year, so the vacation category amount increases. Remember, you must justify every expense. Zero-based budgeting helps you be more disciplined and thus reduce wasteful spending. This philosophy is very popular among personal budgeting gurus.

PAY YOURSELF FIRST

Pay yourself first is another philosophy. Some call this reverse budgeting. Let me explain. When you receive a paycheck, the government takes out taxes first; then, we tend to pay our regular bills like rent and utilities. Next, in our spending plan, we pay for those needed expenses like groceries and gas. These items are routine but can fluctuate every month. The unexpected can suddenly hit us, like car repairs, and the costs of $100 a week on coffee, not to mention, eating out three times a week with friends. In the end, your bank account is left desolate. The idea behind paying yourself first is that we take a certain percentage of our paycheck and put it into savings before the money hits our checking account. Most employers can direct an amount or a percentage to go into your 401k or your savings account before the rest hits your regular bank account. You, or should we say your future, gets paid before you pay your rent. Living off less money is the forced result. But in the end, your savings grows, which is a great benefit.

ENVELOPE METHOD

An oldie but a goodie method is called the envelope method. You may have seen someone reach into a drawer, pull out an envelope with cash in it and take some out before they went shopping. In that drawer, they have several marked envelopes; groceries, gas, coffee, eating out, mad money, or whatever they spend cash on. By the way, having a cash-based system typically saves you money since we tend to spend less with cash than with credit cards. The idea is to cash out your paycheck and divide it into various marked envelopes. We stop spending in that category when we run out of money in that envelope. No cash equals no more spending until we earn another paycheck. Items like rent and car payments are paid by check or direct withdrawal instead of cash. Online programs, like Mvelopes and Goodbudget, mimic this format, so cashing out your paycheck is becoming unnecessary.

PERCENTAGE BUDGETING

Another budgeting philosophy is known as the percentage budget. The idea is to break up your budget using certain percentages for very general categories. This philosophy is designed to help you both focus on living within your means and planning for the future. There are several percentage variations out there.

One variation is the 70-30 rule. The first 30% is evenly split between the three categories: 10% for long-term savings (retirement), 10% for short-term savings (emergencies), and 10% for charity. The remaining 70% is for you to spend how you see fit.

A different breakdown method is the 50-30-20 rule. It is similar to the 70-30 rule but has a little twist on the 70%. You first take 50% for your basic living expenses like rent, gas, and groceries. These are items you need to survive. The following 30% goes to savings, and 20% is spent on whatever you want. Hopefully you can distinguish your needs from your wants since this is critical for success.

AVERAGE BUDGETING

Similar to the percentage budget is what I call the average budget. You find out what the average person spends on a category and try to match that percentage. So, if the average person spends 30% of their income on housing, you shoot for about the same ratio. If you spend 40% of your income on housing, you may have too much house. Then again, you may live in an area where 40% is average since housing is outrageous and moving is not an option. Remember that overspending in one category means sacrifice in another category.

Using the average budget method is a good barometer to measure if we are way off in a category, but budgets are unique and personal. Your season of life can also affect your percentages. Looking at the average is a way to grasp if you are heading in the right direction, but do not try to mimic the average. None of us will ever be average in all our spending categories. This method is really designed to only be a guide. When we get into a sample budget, in chapter 18, I will give you some typical percentages per category. You may also find different variations of this as you search online examples.

A SIDE NOTE:

Each of these philosophies can also be structured by time, like when expenses are due. You will have a couple of main categories. One is monthly expenses. These are items you pay for every month, like rent, food, utilities...Next are the non-monthly expenses. This list will include things you purchase quarterly or annually; items like Christmas, car insurance, annual subscriptions, vacations...

VALUE BASED BUDGETING

As I think of the various philosophies, my purpose driven mind always comes back here. Value Based Budgeting requires more thought and can be a mindset change for some people. You must consider what is most important to you and plan to cover these activities. Your categories are value-based. Some use the terms needs and wants.

You pay your basic living expenses, but you save with a purpose. Whatever temptation grabs your attention, does not steal away your money. You put the money towards that dream that brings inspiration. You can look back with pride and satisfaction, knowing where all your money went and where all your money is going.

Your values affect all your money decisions. If you value travel over where you live, you may buy a small condo instead of a larger house. In this way, you attain extra money to travel. If you value eating healthy, this may cause you to spend more on groceries than eating out. Values promote change in habits, and values require focus.

Let me tell you a story about how we can start with the right vision but take a wrong turn because we lost our focus. For my wife and I, investing in our house is one of our values. We like to make our house a home and make wise upgrades that we both enjoy and increase the value of our house. Interest rates dropped, and it made sense to refinance. We reduced our time frame from a 30-year loan to a 15-year loan, and the monthly payments were not that much higher.

On top of that, we could draw out about $30,000 in cash. We had planned to build an addition to the house and thought this would cover the cost. After more investigation, we realized we needed more than what we anticipated. Instead of adding an addition, we decided to finish off the walk-in attic and make it into our boy's bedroom. We also had two large trees that grew in the middle of the driveway cut down, and we paved the driveway. These things added value to the home. The cost for these projects was $10,000.

So then we had $20,00 left over. Here is where we failed. We lost vision. When our family went to Florida on vacation, we bought a timeshare. Half of the $20 grand was now gone. The other half magically disappeared over the next year. We are not sure where our money went. Our failure to plan caused a failure with our money. It took several years to get rid of the pit in my stomach when I thought about how I spent this money.

Value-based budgeting keeps you focused. You aspire to attain goals specific and unique to you. It's not random; it is purposeful. It's not a cookie-cutter approach because one size does not fit all. You can create better opportunities to help you do what you want.

MIX & MATCH

You will notice an overlap as you look over the different types of budgets. They are all only trying to do the same thing: to help you manage your money. You will probably not choose just one method. You will mix and match what fits best for you. For now, do not be concerned about which budget type fits your need. Your blend will emerge as you get further into this book and investigate how to write your own budget.

As we dive into the various online budgeting programs, you will see that programs like YNAB use zero-based budgeting with a look that fits the envelop method. EveryDollar also uses zero-based budgeting but uses the pay yourself first method. You can pick and choose and find out what works best for you. In the end, it is YOUR budget and YOUR vision, and YOU are the one who is responsible for steering yourself where you want to go.

* * *

As you look over the different budgeting philosophies, what is your order of preference?

(1 being the most preferred, 6 being the least preferred)

_______ Zero based budgeting
_______ Pay Yourself First
_______ Envelope Method
_______ Percentage Budgeting
_______ Average Budgeting
_______ Value Based Budgeting

11

K.I.S.S.

I almost named this book Budget Kiss, but my wife thought most people would not understand what I mean by the word "kiss." K.I.S.S. is more appropriate. It is an acronym created by Kelly Johnson an American aircraft engineer, meaning "Keep It Simple Stupid".[18] One of the main reasons people fail is that budgets tend to grow tedious and complicated with so many categories and options. The bigger the budget gets, the more categories we create, and the more time it requires us to manage our finances. Before we realize what is happening, we are either behind in managing the process or turning into budget nerds constantly looking at our budget app on our phones and giggling whenever we create a new category.

Remember, budgeting is a tool, not an end in itself. We budget to take us somewhere, not budget for the pleasure of seeing how we can rearrange our categories or spending stress-filled hours trying to figure out why our budget is off 12 cents. Now, if you are a budgeting nerd and picked up this book because you read everything with budget in the title, I salute you. You have your passion, and you get budgeting like no one else. But for the rest of us, let's just Keep It Simple for Sam. Instead of stupid, we

[18] https://www.interaction-design.org/literature/article/kiss-keep-it-simple-stupid-a-design-principle#

will just call ourselves "Sam." It sounds so much better.

Let's look at some simple to complex examples in budgeting. The most simplistic budget is the checking account balance method. It compares last month's ending balance to the previous month's balance to see if our account is growing. This is not a budget that most of us can live with. It is too simple and not really managing our money. I had a friend in college that would go to the ATM every week to check his bank balance. This was his budget program. Needless to say, he frequently bounced checks. People who have tried this watch their checking account shrink month to month until they can no longer pay their bills. I think more details are required to enable us to make informed decisions.

On the other hand, having a complex budget with 120 different categories is probably more than our minds can handle. We have to constantly remember which category an item was assigned to and what the purpose of having this category was designed to fulfill. We can become frustrated and confused with all the options. We tend to make errors and eventually trash the budget, starting over at best, or throwing in the towel at worst.

Food is one category that people tend to over-categorize. They split hairs by type, place, people, and even time. Types of food can be the food you cook, the food already cooked, and items that are not food but you purchased with your food when you went to the grocery store. You can buy food at the grocery store, a nice restaurant, a fast-food place, or a coffee shop. You can have food categorized by eating on the go, with your entire family, or on a date night with your spouse or significant other. Your meal may be part of a birthday party, vacation, or another special event. Do you get the picture? All these choices are confusing and much too complicated for me. I like to keep things simple. If you need that much detail, most programs allow you to add notes or place a tag on the purchase. This is much simpler than creating five, six, or ten subcategories and having to decide which category fits best.

Let's take our knife and fork and dig deeper into this food category. For most of us, separating eating in from eating out is a great option. There is a cost difference, and we need to treat them differently since we are managing money. Some call eating in - "Groceries." They also call eating out – "Restaurants." For clarity, take out from a restaurant is not eating in - it is eating out. For those budgeting nerds, please don't freak out: I like things simple, so I include items like soap, paper towels, and other personal items in my grocery budget. These items are on the same receipt, so I keep them in the same category. Coffee at Starbucks is eating out. I think you understand my rationale.

If you find that your category, say eating out, is way too high, you may need to break it down a little further until you get a handle on it. That is where subcategories like restaurants, fast food, and coffee could be helpful. The purpose of a budget is to help you analyze where your money goes so you can redirect your finances to the area you want to grow. If you need to create subcategories within your broad categories to help monitor your spending habits, then do so. Just be careful not to be too carried away. The goal is to avoid being overwhelmed by your budget.

Two questions stand out that we need to ask ourselves before we divide a category.

- Question 1: Is the category descriptive enough, so I know what goes into it and what should not go into it?
- Question Two: Will dividing the category up help me manage my finances better? What I mean by that is, will dividing the category affect how I spend my money? If this enables you to change your

behavior, then this is a positive move in helping you manage your finances.

Besides limiting your categories, you can do a few more things to help you stay on budget and simplify your life.

First, we need to determine what are your necessities, preferences, and desires. Ask yourself, what would I need to live off of for six months if I were a minimalist? Items like eating out, entertainment, travel, some personal products, clothes, gym memberships, and subscriptions... go away. As much as we like them, prefer them, and even desire them - if we had to, we could live without them for six months. Preferences usually deal with brand names. I buy the grocery store brand frosted wheat square cereal versus the Kellogg's Frosted Mini-Wheats, which cost twice as much. Desires are the things I want because I want them, and I struggle to say no to myself. This could be a $5.00 cup of coffee instead of making my own. It could also be driving to work instead of taking the bus. When you obtain clarity with these lines of distinction, you can make the hard decisions more straightforward. You can then align your purchases with your vision and values, and you will be moving closer to your goals.

Another thing you can do to make managing your money simpler is to automate what you can. As we discussed, have your employer deposit the amount you want to save directly into your savings account and the remaining balance into your checking account. After that, ignore your savings account for a few months; believe me, it will grow. If your utility company has the option to bill on average versus actual usage, I recommend you switch to this method. This way, you have the same amount due every month instead of watching it fluctuate with the weather. Having direct withdrawal on specific bills can also help. Make sure they are paid after your paycheck normally gets deposited to ensure you have enough money to cover the payments.

When you start budgeting, you always want to begin with a simple structure and slowly move to the complex. Fewer categories are an excellent place to start, then you can split them up with more subcategories as the need becomes apparent. It is a process, not a destination.

Budgets are not stagnant; they change because we change. Life is full of challenges, opportunities, new experiences, and renewed passions. We grow older and take on more responsibilities. My goodness, as I look back, life has changed so fast. You must focus on your values and let your budget change with your life. But always remember to Keep It Simple Sam.

* * *

List five things (that require money) you can not live without:

____

____

____

____

____

12

The Vortex of Debt

I knew a young couple with three kids under four years of age and one more on the way. They rented a small house in the suburbs. He was employed full-time, and his wife was a stay-at-home mom. At that time, there were few jobs available for stay-at-home moms, so they lived off one income. He made enough to provide the basic needs for the family, but if emergencies like medical bills or car repairs happened, debt became the solution. To cover his debt, my friend decided not to pay taxes. He raised his dependents so high that no federal or state taxes could be withdrawn. He also chose not to file his taxes. He told me he ran across a group with over one million members who signed a form stating they could no longer support a government that used their tax money to support things that went against their conscience. When I heard this, I asked him who his employer was, and he told me he worked for the state. I said that this was an interesting dilemma. Anyway, my point is that debt can cause us to make some decisions that are just not rational.

Debt can be a heavy burden. I hate debt. Maybe it's pride, having to admit I need help with this purchase. Perhaps it's the thought that I lost some of my freedom. I am now tied to this institution that I owe money. As the bumper sticker said, "I owe, I owe, so off to work I go." I would be going off to work anyway, but the thought that I was working so someone else could withdraw part of my paycheck bothers me. Debt can limit our options and puts pressure on us to work with creative financing, like "Robbing Peter to pay Paul" or, more precisely, robbing Uncle Sam to pay Bank of America.

Even though I hate debt, I also understand that some debt can be good. Think of it as two people coming together to accomplish something that one person can not do alone. When my wife and I first got married, we rented an apartment. At the end of one year, we had saved enough money for a down payment on a house. Owning a home is far better financially since we receive something back for the money we pay. Bit by bit, we own more of the house; while renting for a year, we got nothing. It would have taken me a lifetime to save enough money to buy a home. Not only would our rent keep going up, but the price of a house would also be going up. The solution was to borrow from a bank.

Types of Debt

There are different types of debt. Consumable debt is when you borrow money, but you soon realize you have nothing to show for it. Credit card purchases fit this category. We buy things and consume the product. We purchased food we did not enjoy, clothes we never wore, and miscellaneous items that are boxed away in storage. Thirty days later we get the bill not remembering half of what is on it. The other kind of debt gives us items that last much longer. A car or a house fits this category. This debt is more acceptable since these items hold their value and use much longer.

Getting a loan on a car is a little more debatable. A house usually increases in value every year. As for vehicles, they typically go down in value. Besides seasonal adjustments, I only remember one time when housing values went down. I can recall only one time in my life when used car values have gone up. You can see the trend, houses appreciate, and cars depreciate. This is especially true when you buy a new car. Some say when you drive a new car off the lot, its value drops 20%. Unless you are doing a lot of driving, and dependability on the vehicle is crucial, most of us can purchase a less expensive used car and pay cash rather than buying a new vehicle that ties up our cash flow for five or more years. If you must obtain a loan, pay it off in two or three years. When your car ages, your repairs also grow. You do not want to have significant car repairs and car payments happening at the same time. This can strain your budget.

Credit card debt is the worst kind of debt you can accumulate. Interest is at a high rate and keeps building and building. In the end, that vacation you enjoyed cost you $2,000 in credit card debt. With monthly payments, it ended up costing over $3,000 and took you over five years to pay off. If you only made the minimum required payment (18% interest with 2% minimum)it would take over 24 years to pay off your debt. You may not mind the payments for the first year, but after that, you will kick yourself every month you make a payment. Interest accumulates daily. So each day, your balance is not just your purchases, but the interest owed from the day before. Think of it as paying interest on the interest. Ouch! The thing about credit cards is once you start using them and build debt, you keep using them. You forget about the total amount due and focus on the minimum payments. You get hooked, and off to work you go because you owe, owe, owe.

If credit card debt does not scare you yet, look at some statistics.

- American households have $841 billion in credit card debt in 2022 (leandingtree.com).
- Average household credit card debt is over $5000 (2021 Experian.com).
- The average household has 2.3 credit cards (Valuepenguin.com).
- About 45% of Americans carry credit card debt balances (Debt.com).
- The average credit card interest rate is 18.7% and rising in 2022 (Washington Post, Oct 17 2022).
- According to the National Bureau of Economics Research, between 9 % and 20% pay the minimum balance due on their credit cards.

These statistics are not listed to shame you or validate that you are in the majority. They are to show you how our culture has been tricked by the big financial institutions so that they can take your hard-earned money away. You become a slave to your lender. More and more of your paycheck goes to them and limits your future.

If a credit card is used correctly and with self-control, it can benefit you. For those with no credit, you can build good credit by spending less than 1/3 of your credit limit and paying the entire balance off every month. You can even obtain a credit card with points or cash back. I pay everything I can on my credit card and pay it off in full every month. The cashback pays for a vacation for my family every other year. The key is ensuring you have the money in the bank before using the credit card. You can also set up your credit card to automatically draft the balance due from your checking account. In this way, you never miss paying off what you owe.

If you lack the discipline to pay off your credit card every month, then stay away from them. Use cash or debit cards for your purchases and keep good records. Credit cards are convenient, but people tend to spend more with credit cards since they do not connect the money they have in the bank with the money they are spending. The money you use from a credit card is not yours; it is a loan that must be paid back.

The biggest thing about debt is that it robs you of your future by making you pay for your past. Your future money is now tied up paying for your past purchases. When you do not use credit, it becomes satisfying to experience the outcome of using the money you earned and not depending on others to help with your purchase. You can remember what you did without regrets. You can be pleased with your purchase and not carry this nagging pit in your stomach, wondering why you did what you did and how you will pay for this burden.

Paying off Debt

How do you deal with debt? The obvious answer is to pay off what you owe and not incur any more debt. Live within your means, or the mean debt collector will take everything away. If you acquired a lot of different obligations, you might want to research to find out if you can consolidate them with a loan that gives you a lower interest rate. One debt will make it easier to manage and more straightforward to budget. If consolidation is not available or practical, you can follow one of two thoughts in paying off debt.

The first is to focus on the debt with the highest interest rate. You make the minimum payment for all your creditors except for the one with the highest interest rate. You can then pay a more considerable amount for this high-interest creditor. In the long run, this method will save you the most money. If one of your most significant debts is also one of your biggest, this process can make you feel the weight of the upward battle since it seems to take a long time to pay it off.

Another way to pay off your debt is to go after the smallest one first. In this way, the number of creditors you have begins to shrink, and you receive encouragement to keep going. Motivation is vital when you amass a mountain of debt. I had a friend that walked through this method. After a few short months, you could observe how encouraged he was and how his confidence in slaying the debt monster had grown. Eliminating all the small debts first certainly motivates you so you can tackle the big ones.

The idea of eliminating the small debt first creates a snowball effect. When one debt is paid off, you take that money that you used to pay off this debt and add it to the minimum payment you were making on the next smallest debt. When that one is eliminated, you can add that amount to the next debt and so on.

If you are disciplined, you may want to focus on the higher interest rates first. If you are like most people and would love to see the number of creditors reduced, concentrate on the lower amounts first. There is no correct answer on which to choose. The point is that you are moving forward in reducing your debt.

Conclusion

If your budget does not allow you to meet your debt obligations, you need to look for options. First, do not ignore your creditors. Answer their phone calls, respond to their letters. In this way, they will be more willing to work with you. Even if you can pay $15.00 a month, they will take it and it will reduce the chance of them coming after you. This will give you time to seek help, get a part time job, or talk to a credit specialist who may have other options for you.

When all your debts are paid off, you will feel a weight lifted off your shoulders. That is the feeling of freedom and accomplishment that arises when you are debt free. If you compile debt, you carry the weight. The burden slowly builds. You feel it there, but you do not realize the toll it takes on your mind and body. Anxiety about money can cause you to sleep poorly, have panic attacks, make you feel isolated, and even affect your ability to think clearly. When stress is not dealt with, your blood pressure, immune system, and memory are affected. Avoiding it only causes more stress. It's time to move life forward and fight for your financial freedom. Life rarely takes enormous leaps forward. One baby step at a time produces great progress in the long term. You can overcome debt, and the results will bring you freedom.

* * *

List all your debts:

Lender	Amount	Date Due	Minimum payment

13

Cultivating The Future

A few years ago, we purchased a wonderful home with a fenced in flower garden behind the house. You can tell the previous owner took great care of their garden with the colorful blooms emerging at various seasons. However, the front of the house was a little more rustic; no grass, overgrown bushes, full of trees. You could say it had more of a "natural look" to it. I was shocked at how many leaves fell during our first fall in the house. Personally, I like cutting grass rather than raking a whole lot of leaves. Did I mention the trees dropped nuts as well?There were too many to count. After one season of leaf raking and nut collecting, we decided to cut down a few trees, approximately 30. We brought in topsoil and planted grass seed. Year after year, we planted various bushes and flowering trees to develop the landscaping. At first, the plants were small, and the grass was sparse. But through hard work and patience, the grass thickened up, the azaleas bloomed, and a beautiful landscape emerged.

Just like the process of developing a beautiful yard, we can cultivate a future through the practice of savings. If debt is robbing the future to pay for the past, then saving is postponing the present to pay for the future.

Saving says, "There is someplace I want to go, and the only way I can get there is to sacrifice something now." You do this because you possess a vision of a future for yourself and your family that is better than what you are currently experiencing. Motivation to change happens because you are unsatisfied with your current situation and you recognize the sacrifices that will move you closer to that better life.

Savings may be a general category but specific goals need to be listed as your subcategories. These are developed with a purpose and involve various steps.

The first step in savings is to grow an emergency fund. Think of this as the grass that holds the dirt in place when a storm comes. Without the grass, the pouring rain creates gullies through your yard, washing away all your topsoil. I literally had this happen when I first planted grass seed. The very next day, the rains came pouring down and the seed floated away with some of my new topsoil. After this, the neighbor had some great looking green grass.

We all know life happens. Things break down; needs arise. We live in a world where nothing lasts forever, and we need to plan for it. A couple of months ago, my daughter went to the dentist. Her teeth were fine except for the fact that she had too many. Her wisdom teeth were coming in. If they were not removed, she would have serious problems. The cost was over $2500. Because we had a savings fund, I was not stressed. Was I happy? No. But the care of my daughter will always be more important than the bank account balance. The emergency fund was set up for emergencies, just like this.

An emergency fund can be as little as $1000 or as much as six months of expenses. These savings are designed to grow and provide for specific needs. Emergency funds are for emergencies. Sounds logical. However, before we move forward, we need to define what an emergency is. It is not a birthday party or a vacation. It is not even for regular maintenance on your car. It is for things that unexpectedly come up and that must be cared for, or something worse will happen. These emergencies can be medical, large car or house repairs, or a loss of income.

The next type of savings is for planned events. I liken them to the bushes we planted. I had a specific look I want for my front yard, and I laid out each plant to satisfy that impression. Your planned events are the bills that you expect to happen sometime in the near future. They are not unexpected but regular events. If your car insurance is due every six months, save monthly for it. By the way, most insurance companies allow you to pay monthly. Your family's birthdays and Christmas always happen at the same time every year. You may take a vacation every year around the same time. Plan for it in your budget. That means you need to save something every month so that when the event happens, you have the money to pay for it. I also include car maintenance in this category. Historically, I need to save about $150 a month for car repairs. Besides regular oil changes, I know that one large bill will come at me annually, like tire replacement or the repair of some item on the car whose purpose is beyond my comprehension. I plan for this, so I am not concerned when it happens. Events you know will take place do not need to sneak up on you. Save monthly, and you will be blessed with the money to cover these expenses. By doing so, stress is reduced, and peace is maintained.

The next phase of savings is your wish list. These are like the flowering crepe myrtles I planted. They may take a few years to develop but eventually they produce beautiful white and red blossoms. Everybody's wish list is different. For my 15-year-old son, it is a car. For my 29-

year-old daughter, it may be a house. For me, it looks more like a long trip with my wife. At the present time, these items are financially out of reach, but if you do not start taking steps now, you will never experience reaching your goal. A journey begins with small steps. In this process, obstacles will come, and setbacks will hit you. Keep going with your vision in front of you, and eventually, you will reap its blessing.

The last step in savings is retirement. For some of you, this is so far in the future that you can't even comprehend it. It is like planting that oak tree that you hope will one day shade your house from the summer sun. Every book you read on budgeting says to plan on it. Retirement will happen unless you die early in life, so start saving for it. For the young reader, all it takes is a little, and the magic of compound interest will amaze you. I have heard stories of blue-collar workers not making much more than minimum wage their whole life but retiring as millionaires because they saved early and saved often. Retiring rich is not a product of the smart but the result of a disciplined and consistent behavior.

Are you overwhelmed with all of this? I sure am. Too many categories to save for and not enough money can be daunting. If you tried to save for each of these simultaneously, you may not be able to pay your essential bills. The trick is to focus on one at a time, like starting with some grass seed and every year adding a bush or two. Start with an emergency fund, and then focus on a plan for specific annual needs. The next is to set aside some small amount for retirement and the rest towards that big purchase. Remember, you are not in a sprint but a marathon. Good things come to those who wait. Waiting is not passive; it actively engages in life and in your spending patterns.

It is time to act, to plan, and take steps forward. You can stand up to the storms that are coming. In the end, the rains may fall, but you will not be washed away. The waters may rise, but you will be firmly rooted, and then you will experience the joy of overcoming the challenge rather than seeing your dreams swept away with all of your topsoil.

* * *

Below is a list of possible savings funds. First, number them in the order of importance. Next, fill out an amount you would like to have in each fund and the monthly contribution you need to make to reach that amount.

Saving Categories

Category	Monthly Contribution	Savings Goals
Emergency Fund		
Birthdays/Gifts		
Christmas		
Vacation		
Non-Monthly Expenses		
Retirement		
Wish 1: ____________________		
Wish 2: ____________________		
Wish 3: ____________________		

Be sure to write out specific non-monthly expenses

14

Pitfalls To Budgeting

Recently I tried a new online program. I wanted to start my budget from scratch, so I glanced over my expenses, created the various categories, figured out my monthly income, and divided it among all my expenses. I thought the budget looked good. My plan made sense, and I felt comfortable with the outcome. Once a week, I went into the program, categorized each new transaction, and analyzed how my budget worked out. Week 1 looked great. Week 2 was awesome. Week three went by without a hitch. Next came week four. I had an expense that did not fit any category. My health insurance bill happened! How could I have missed such an obvious expense? This is not an expense you can simply work in. Needless to say, I had to redo the budget.

We make mistakes. We cannot plan for everything. We do not know the future. Life is constantly changing. These are not reasons to give up. They are challenges to overcome. This chapter will help you see some pitfalls that could happen if you are not careful.

Mindset

The first pitfall to budgeting is your mindset. Most of this was covered in the Why section, but it is so important that we need to reiterate it. We need to change a failure mindset to a success mindset. Put aside those thoughts that that tell you that this is too hard. Silence that voice that says you cannot do it. Take one step at a time. Do what you can do today, and don't let your mind drift down the path of worst-case scenarios.

You need to give yourself grace. Understand that we all make mistakes and waste money. We have all gone through buyer's remorse. We can't change the past. The focus needs to be on what we need to do now with what we possess now. Beating yourself up will gain you nothing except further despair. As someone once said to me, stop listening to yourself and start speaking to yourself. Tell yourself what you can do, not what you can't do. You can do this. Retain a mindset that speaks to success, and you will start walking in it.

Safety Net

Another pitfall to budgeting is not having a safety net. Dave Ramsey, the author of The Total Money Makeover[19], created seven baby steps to financial peace. The very first step is to create a $1,000 emergency fund. It is worth noting that debt reduction is not first in these seven baby steps; it is second. You need an emergency fund to help you stop the cycle of relying on debt. Having the ability to borrow whenever you want gives you a false sense of security that can quickly spiral into a vortex that swallows up all your financial plans.

Emergencies happen. This is life. Medical expenses, home repairs, and larger-than-planned car repairs are only a few things that can happen. The third step in Dave's program is to save 3 to 6 months of expenses in a savings account. This is to give you that safety net for more significant

[19] Ramsey, Dave. The Total Money Makeover, 2003 Thomas Nelson Publishers

unexpected emergencies like a loss of income. Dave Ramsey's Financial Peace University program is excellent. I highly recommend it.

Non-Monthly Expenses

Failure to budget non-monthly expenses can be another pitfall in budgeting. Most people think of items like car insurance which comes every six months, or Christmas, which comes once a year. These expenses can be more attainable if you put aside money every month rather than playing catch up or relying on debt. By the way, don't plan on that Christmas bonus to pay for the Christmas presents. One downturn in the economy or a change in management, and "Shazam", that bonus has somehow disappeared. Always plan on what you have, not what you could possibly earn.

Lifestyle

Life changes, and so does our lifestyle. I went from being single to being married. After a year and a half, we were a family of three, and my wife stopped working her corporate job. During that same time, we bought a house, and I received two promotions. Eighteen months later, we grew into a family of four. Three years later, our family expanded to five and we needed a bigger h ouse. Promotions came, expenses increased, and our expectations of how we wanted to live changed. We wanted nicer clothes and cars. We wanted the best toys and education for our kids. As I look back on this, I can see how the rat race changed our perspectives and encouraged us to drift away from our plans. Some changes are not bad in themselves, but a budget is needed to ensure you live within your income. A plan is needed, or you will drift away from your why, and your values will fall away in the busyness of life.

As life changes, your why and your values may also change. The point is that you need to recognize they change and that you agree with the change. Sometimes things just happen, and you need to adjust. Other times you plan on changing things because you have changed.

My wife and I decided to have another child almost eight years after our third child was born. We chose to make this change and planned for it. After our new daughter turned one, we decided we were done having children. We were older and, frankly, getting tired. A couple of weeks after we made this decision, we found out we were pregnant with our fifth child. This was an unexpected bonus baby. We did not plan this. It just happened. Well, we all know how it happened, but it was not in our plan. Fast forward 15 years, and my wife and I can tell you that we are extremely blessed by this fifth child. Our youngest two are best friends, and the two of them have helped keep our other children connected to us. The two of them opened doors for us that we would have not experienced without either one of them. The joy our children bring us is irreplaceable. The fifth child may not have been on our plan, but God had a better plan. It is important to remember, we make a plan, hold it loosely, learn to be flexible, and adjust to life's changes while always staying true to our values. Because of these unexpected changes, our why has become more evident, and our values have grown more solid.

Here is a note of caution on our spending habits and lifestyle changes. As we make more, we tend to spend more. As we spend more, we tend to want more. As we want more, we fail to focus on our values and gravitate towards the instant rather than the meaningful. As a friend of mine once told me, "The more you own, the more that owns you."

Instant Gratification

Nothing derails a budget more than needing instant gratification. We are attracted to something we want, and we make the purchase. Shopping in a mall without a specific purpose can be the worse enemy of a budget. My wife and I went to the mall to walk around and do some window shopping. We entered a big department store, and I drifted to the men's clothes as she looked in the woman's section. I saw a green shirt I liked. My office was going more casual in dress, and this shirt would help me fit in well. I bought it. When I got home, I hung it up in the closet, only to find that I had another similar shirt. Now I had two green shirts that fit the casual attire: Oh joy! (Sarcasm)

Instant gratification temps us all the time. When we surf the web, go to the grocery store, and get bombarded with email advertisements with all sorts of promises, we are tempted to spend money. One area we always tend to compromise is the category called food. We go to the grocery store without a plan for what to eat. We fail to plan dinner, so we order takeout. It is so much easier to give in and buy rather than think about our budget. We all need to eat, right?

One trick to help delay gratification is to make a list of what you want and wait a week before you buy it. I created a "Not Dad's Wish List" on Amazon. When I am drawn to something I like, I put it on my wish list. I wait a few days to see if this is a need or a preference. I tend to forget about it until I see something else to add to my list. At this point, I delete a few older items that I realized I did not need, and I no longer wanted. I just saved a ton of money. If I believe I still need them and I maintain money in my budget, I can now buy them. My conscience is clear, and my purchase is wise. I purchased with thought, not impulse. My purchase is satisfying and without regret. The next time you are tempted to buy, tell yourself you will revisit this after a certain amount of time has passed. Occasionally you may miss a deal, but you will feel much better knowing you made an informed purchase.

Everyone wants a part of your money, but you are the gatekeeper, and your budget is the door. Do not let the seller jump over the fence and take the money you plan to spend on something else.

A Loss of Meaning

The last pitfall I want to cover is not working the budget you developed. On one extreme, you can completely ignore the budget you created. Basically, you are living without a budget. You made one, but you rarely look at it. You may even enter new transactions, but you did not compare your spending to what you planned to spend. Your budget serves no purpose except to offer false comfort that you have one. There is no connection between your budget and your purpose.

The less subtle form of not working the budget is letting your expenses drive your budget instead of your values. Every month you adjust your budget to match your spending patterns without any form of evaluation. Eventually, the budget becomes a record of what happened instead of a plan to take you somewhere. It has become a history book. Budgeting then becomes meaningless. You do the exercise because you are supposed to. This is what responsible people do, right? Budgets are a plan for the future, not merely a record of the past. They are a road map to where you want to be in five years and beyond.

Summary:

You can take these reasons for failure along with a list of others and summarize them in one of three camps.

- The first is that we failed to plan. We did not think through all the issues that awaited us. It's not that we can anticipate everything, but we need to realize the unplannable is coming.
- The next camp is losing our focus on our why. We can get caught up with so many distractions calling our name. Remember what

you truly value. Stay focused, and you will overcome obstacles and achieve your goals.

- The last camp is the most dangerous. It is giving up. You no longer feel like your dreams are possible. You have too many obstacles. You tried and failed too many times. It's time to hit the reset button and revisit your why. It's time to get help and seek counsel. We are never called to walk alone. We are called to a community. There are no Lone Rangers in the world. If you remember the TV show, you know that even the Lone Ranger had Tonto.

* * *

What is your biggest pitfall to not succeeding in a budget?

____

____

____

____

IV

HOW

"Budget – a mathematical confirmation of your suspicions"

– A. A. Lattimer

15

Yesterday's Money

One summer, my wife and two of my kids had the opportunity to go to China with a group of people from the United States. When we were in Beijing, we visited a mall that was 14 floors h igh. As we came in, we could look up and see the vastness of the building. Shops and people were everywhere. Stairs, elevators, and escalators seemed to zig-zag throughout the complex. The group split up to explore the shops and then meet at a restaurant after a couple of hours. This place was big and confusing. One thing I look for when I do not know where I am going is a map. When I found a map of the mall, I realized I could not read Chinese. Even so, I could figure out where I had been and then determined where I was by the map's design. Once I knew where I was on the map, I could figure out where I needed to go.

Mapping out your budget begins with your financial history. Just like my Chinese map story, your history helps you determine where you currently are. Your past gives you a look into your present situation. You need to know where you are to determine how to get to where you want to go. The money you earned yesterday helps you predict what your income will be tomorrow.

It's time to take a step back and gather data. You cannot create a budget unless you know your income and expenses. Do a little gathering expedition. For some of you, this may be as easy as looking at your checking account. For others, you have no idea where to begin. You can get your latest pay stub to help determine income. If you have various income streams, you may need to go through the deposits in your checking account. What you need is your take home pay, not your estimated income before taxes.

Let me tell you a story...

Sally made about $36,000 a year. She wanted to be diligent with her money, so she created a budget. It took her a couple of weeks to gather all her historical spending trends and determine what categories to put them in. She wanted to prove to herself that she could do it, and she even used Excel to create a spreadsheet to keep track of it all. With the budget completed, she was proud of her spreadsheet and the various color schemes she used for different spending groups. It looked fantastic.

A month later, Sally came to a friend discouraged. At the end of the month, she was about $380 short. Sally looked tired and angry. She had worked so hard, and it all made sense until she started recording her income and expenses. Her bank account and her budget did not match up. She tried for hours to reconcile them but to no avail. Confusion and frustration were her result.

Her friend looked over her budget and realized that Sally left off one expense that worked out to $380. This expense was not in her budget because it came out of her paycheck before it hit her bank. That expense is called taxes. Sally budgeted her income based on her salary before the government took their money. Her employer told her she makes

$36,000 a year, which equals $3,000 a month. This is true, but Uncle Sam takes his share first - $380 a month. Look at your paycheck to determine your take-home pay. After-tax-income is the income you use to budget, not your total salary before taxes.

For some people calculating your take-home pay is easy. They are on a salary and receive the same amount for every paycheck. The calculation gets a bit harder if you are hourly or on commission, or you do contract or seasonal work. Timing is the issue.

For those who receive 1099's verses W2's, remember to put in savings the taxes you will owe. If you do not, remember, Uncle Sam always gets his money.

Calculating monthly income becomes very simple if you get paid monthly or twice a month. For those who receive a paycheck every two weeks, for ten months you will receive two paychecks, and for two months, you will receive three. Plan a budget that does not need these extra two paychecks. The months you receive the additional check, use half of it for items like food and gas since these represent more weekly expenses, and then save the balance. You will be proud of yourself later.

For those with inconsistent income, the simplest way to calculate your monthly income is to take your estimated after-tax annual income and divide it by twelve. Remember, this is after you paid your income taxes, not before. You assume you will make the same this year as last year, so try to be conservative in your calculation. It is fantastic news when you end up with more money than you planned, but it can also be disastrous if you end up with less money than you budgeted. Part of the goal is to take the stress out of life, not add more.

Contract, self-employed, and seasonal workers have more difficulty creating a budget. It takes much more focus and self-discipline. For you, I think of the proverb that talks about the ant. The ant gathers its food in the summer so it can live comfortably in the winter.[20] You have to be a good ant when it comes to budgeting. Savings is the key to success here.

When calculating your income, ignore bonuses, gifts, and unusual commissions earned. These are not normal. They can skew your results and cause you to spend it before you receive it.

When I was a little child, I remember when my family bought a new car. I was excited to go somewhere and sit in the back seat taking in the view and absorbing that new car smell. Purchasing this car was made possible because my dad would receive a significant bonus every year. The last few years, it was like clockwork: the same big bonus, the same amount. One year, he did not get that bonus. He told me several stories of his coworkers that were financially in trouble because they spent their bonus money before they had received it. A bonus is not a promise and is not secure. It is an extra – not a guarantee. Don't count your chickens before they hatch.

Before we move on to the expense categories, I want to put up a couple of warning signs. The goal is to stay on budget and not allow unexpected income to cause you to take a detour. If you get a bonus from work or receive a random cash gift, do not spend it. Take a small portion and celebrate. For the rest of the money, save it. This unexpected boost in your cash flow can help propel you closer to your goal and increase your motivation to keep moving forward. It will be like getting your second wind while running a long race.

---

[20] Proverbs 6:8

A word to the wise: The more you make, the more you spend. Without realizing it, your desires and your needs somehow match your income. When we make more, we spend more.

So here is my challenge: no matter how much you make these next twelve months, stick to the plan, stay on budget, and resist the temptation to spend. This is where your why and your values protect you. They will keep your eyes on the prize so you can live without regrets.

* * *

Assignment:

1. Gather your last few page stubs, checking account information, and even last years W2's or 1099's.
2. As you look over the last 3 to 6 months of income, is anything not normal, like extra overtime, bonus money, gifts? If so, do not include that in regular income.
3. List all regular income by month over the last 3 months. Average them out. If you do seasonal work, you may need to expand the time frame. Look over the average and ask your self if this is the amount you expect per month over the next six months. If so, you have your income!
4. If you expect to make less than the current average, factor that in. If you expect to make more, be conservative in your estimate.
5. What income will you use to make your budget? ________________

16

The History of Expenses

No, this is not about the history of humanity's spending, but the history of your spending. Before creating categories for your budget, we need to know where your money currently goes. History shows us our habits. Some habits are good and some practices, well, let's just say they need to change.

Tony did not make much money but always paid his bills on time. He felt he was a responsible young man who did OK with his money. If you asked Tony how much money he made, he would probably say he made enough to get by. Tony lived paycheck to paycheck. He rented a house with three other guys. He worked at a coffee shop and did odd jobs occasionally. He was in a band and loved hanging out with his friends.

When Tony turned 30, something happened. He realized his life was going nowhere. He had nothing and doing the same old thing for the last decade revealed he had no actual plans for his life. Thirty seems to be that magic number that wakes us up and causes us to evaluate where we are in life and where we are headed. Maybe it's that age that makes us realize we are now adults.

Tony realized that he could not change his life overnight. It would take time, so he decided to start one step at a time. Tony was wiser than he looked. He looked at his W2 and his current paycheck to determine his income. Next was his expenses. He had no credit cards, no debt, and most of his other expenses were shared with the other guys in the house. Then he realized he had a problem. Most of the time, he paid cash for everything. He had a bank account with a couple of hundred dollars in it. But he gave his roommate cash for the rent and utilities. He paid cash for groceries or pizza. He paid cash for gas. He had no receipts or any idea where his money went. He was historically blind.

If you are like Tony, finding your historical expenses will be more like a scavenger hunt. You may have a general idea of what goes where, but the specific amounts will be determined as life progresses. For the rest of us, we need to look at our credit card statements and bank accounts. Three months' history is a good place to start. Remember, what we are looking for first is your regular monthly expenses. You can estimate for now if you do not have an exact amount. A budget is never static. You work at the budget to make it work for you.

Your non-monthly expenses are what throw off budgets more than anything. We know these expenses will happen, but we tend to focus on the urgent which overshadows the reasonable. Take a moment and look around you. What do you possess that needs maintenance or repairs on a regular bases? Do you have a house, a car, a piece of equipment that requires maintenance? Do you have a business or a side job where supplies need to be replenished? Do you have any travel plans, or classes you desire to take? How about anniversaries, birthdays and Christmas? All of these things take money and require you to save up for them over time. You can start by making this list.

If you need more help, chapter 18 will list some specific categories and these may help trigger your memory. As you discover what you are spending it will help if you write down the amounts spent and the date these bills are due. You will need this later. Gather all your expenses together so we can look at putting them in groups or categories.

* * *

Assignment:

1. Gather all your credit card statements, bank statements, cash receipts. Anything that tells you what you have been spending.
2. Three months of information will work, but remember non-monthly and annual expenses.
3. Start listing the date of purchase, the vendor, what it was for, and the amount.
4. Note: doing this in a spreadsheet like excel or google will make it easier. Your bank and credit card transactions can also be downloaded into a CSV file to be used in a spreadsheet.

Expense Spreadsheet Sample

Date	Vendor	Description	Amount

17

The Big Picture

In a previous life, I was the lead on a multi-million dollar building project. When the team met with the architect, he took us through the project's big picture. We looked at the size of the property, the various needs of the facility, the flow of traffic, and the impression we wanted to communicate to the people who drove by our building. These discussions produced a general idea on what we needed. The specifics like trim work, flooring, landscaping, and furniture came later. The big picture gave us the framework and a place for the details to fall.

As we look at expenses, our big picture is our major categories. This will determine how you want to view your budget. It is your philosophy on budgeting. There are a couple of ways you can divide divide up major categories. Some do it by time – monthly, non-monthly, annually. Some do it by value- like needs and wants. Some do it by purpose - housing, transportation...

My philosophy is to budget by purpose and with a purpose. If your money is supposed to take you somewhere, it must have a reason to get there. To me, needs and wants are part of the purpose, so my values help clarify these.

Are you confused yet? Let's get started and see if the fog lifts.

First, you need to figure out your o bligations. Your past decisions go far beyond the past. These decisions affect your present and, to a certain extent, your future. I was a sales manager for an office supply company and part of my responsibility was to visit our customers, attend luncheons, and bring my sales representatives to different e vents. I needed a nice car that would be dependable and give a particular image to the customer and my staff. The result was a sizable car payment that affected my budget. My decision to purchase this car was a decision in my past, but it affected where I could spend money now and where I would spend it over the next couple of years. Things became tight and our debt was not being reduced. Finally after 18 months, my wife and I decided to get serious with our debt and we sold the car.

What obligations do you have? What contracts have you made? What promises do you need to keep? Your word is important because it defines who you are. Do you have debt? Write it down. Do you have a lease agreement? Write it down. Do you owe someone money? Write it down. Not paying them back is not an option. The money you budget for these items has an essential purpose; showing the world and yourself that you are a person of your word and someone who is dependable. Paying them back is something that you can be proud of.

After you have determined your obligations, you can focus on your basic needs. We all need housing, food, transportation, medical, and clothes. With society changing so much over the last couple of decades, items that were once called luxuries are now called necessities. These items can include cell phones, computers, and an internet connection. Our jobs and where we live determine how much we spend on these.

Creative idea! My daughter was on a tight budget and needed internet for work. She could not afford a monthly internet bill for her apartment, so she improvised. Her cell phone plan was unlimited, and she could use it as a hot spot. This enabled her to work from home and incur no extra expense.

For those of you who are self-employed or have a side business, add a category called business. Your business and your personal expenses should always be kept separate.

I treat savings as a specific main category because I always want this category to remind me of my goals. Savings is where you will see your values and your vision for life come into existence: emergency funds, a down payment on a house, a big trip, or starting a business. This is the category of dreams. You can even call it your dream category.

Other general categories can include entertainment and miscellaneous. These must be watched since so many things can find there way here and make it hard to manage.

Your categories will start very general, and as you analyze your spending more specific subcategories will evolve. The general categories can fit just about everyone, but the specific categories will become as unique to you are your values are.

Your budget is made to fit you and your goals. So, if these major categories do not fit your lifestyle, then change them. Some might not spend much on clothing, so they put this under miscellaneous. Others may value travel so much that they make this a major category. It all depends on you.

Some people create a general category called debt since it is a major problem for them. Personally, I do not do this since I want all purchases to have a purpose, and any debt I have must fit in one of my other categories. If I owe money on my house, this debt goes under housing. If I owe money on my car, this debt goes under transportation. Consumer debt is the worst since I have no idea where it should be classified. You may want to create a specific category for this, or you may want to add it under miscellaneous. When I see it under miscellaneous, I realize I have nothing to show for these purchases. My goal is to eliminate debt. That is another reason I do not create a major category for this. Remember that budgets are personal and flexible, so develop a budget that works best for you.

To summarize, here is a suggestion on where to begin with general categories:

-Housing
-Food
-Transportation
-Medical
-Clothing
-Giving
-Entertainment
-Miscellaneous
-Savings
-Business

Ten categories should be about the maximum you would want to have. Remember, the more you have, the more you need to manage. The more you need to manage, the more difficult it becomes. The more difficult it becomes, the more time it consumes. Unless you are a budget nerd, too much time can equal too much to handle, and the temptation to frustration and to even quit will come knocking at your door.

* * *

Assignment:

1. Take the list of expenses you created and write down next to each expenses the general category that best fits that expense.
2. Sort your list by category and then by vendor within each category and then by date.

Expenses Major Category Sample

Date	Vendor	Description	Amount	Major Category
June 15	Food King	groceries	112.58	Food
June 5	Pub Master	friends eating out	29.00	Food
June 22	Big Mart	Jackie's birthday	21.42	Giving
June 10	AC Power	electric	119.00	Housing
June 2	WWW Connect	internet	83.08	Housing
July 1	WWW Connect	internet	83.08	Housing
June 16	GoGoGas	gas	39.42	Transportation

18

Detailing The Details

I like coffee. I have at least two cups every morning. I am an early riser, so when I get my first cup of coffee, everyone else in the house is sound asleep. A few years ago, I picked up the perfect size mug at a shop in the smoky mountains. I fill my cup with a brew of freshly ground coffee and sit back in my rocking chair, looking out the window at our garden. Nothing is more relaxing than the smooth feeling of a great cup of coffee filling my insides with warmth. Coffee is a simple pleasure in life.

As much as I like coffee, I do not have it as a budget category. I tried an online budgeting program that had a large number of predetermined budget items that they assumed everyone needed. There were a lot of categories—too many for my purposes. In fact, over half of the categories, I would never use. The problem came when I could not delete these categories, so I constantly had to scan through them all to find the category I needed. One of these categories I could not delete was coffee. If you are one of these people who spends a couple of hundred dollars a month on coffee, then you probably need a category for this expense. For the rest of us, too many categories can become too confusing and time-consuming. You need to manage the data, not swim in it.

It is important to get specific enough to track spending but not so detailed that we cannot keep up with it. I classify my spending by purpose. Let's look at housing. Money is used to pay my house debt (Mortgage); it is used for outside resources (Utilities), and I budget an amount every month to keep it up to date (Maintenance). If I wanted to save for improvements, I could add another category here, but I prefer to have that under savings since making my house a home is a value to me.

Some people like to break out more categories like gas/electric, then water/sewer, another is trash pickup, and don't forget about cable/internet/landline. I like to keep it simple. I use one category called Utilities for all of these. I can always run a report by the vendor and see what each is costing me. This may freak some budgeters out, but I also put my cell phone and internet in this category. Phones used to be connected with the house (a landline), and my cable/internet certainly is. It is also the same monthly amount, so I know how it affects things.

Your subcategories need to focus on items you need help with, which enables you to be goal specific. Two categories that tend to break people's budgets are food and that mysterious category called "miscellaneous." Food can be divided into groceries and restaurants: eating in or eating out. It is all eating. Food is more than fuel for the body; it is a pleasure, a way to socialize, and a means to connect with people and create community. With it, we stay healthy, and with too much of it, we need a gym membership to take care of the excess. Food is a needed pleasure that requires balance.

Some people like to get too complicated with this food category because it can quickly get out of hand. I covered most of this in chapter 11 K.I.S.S., so I will only tell you that you need to plan what you spend. Do not go to the store hungry, and stick to the list of what you need to buy. If your grocery bill is high and the issue is not inflation, then you may need to break down your purchases into more categories, or at least keep your receipts and review what is on them.

Eating out can also be split in several ways. You can have coffee, date night, fast food, restaurants, time with friends, family night out... You can get as creative as you want but remember, the more categories you have, the more you must manage. K.I.S.S. – keep it simple Sam is what I keep telling myself.

I think I like only having two categories for food: groceries and restaurants.

The problem with a miscellaneous category is that it can quickly develop into a black hole that swallows money and the ability to track it. But you need it since there are items you just can not anticipate and do not fit into any category. For example, my daughter uses my Amazon account from time to time. The other day she made a purchase but failed to change the ship-to address, so it arrived at my doorstep. When I picked up the package, I noticed that her name was on it, so I took a picture and texted it to her. Oops, was her reply. She lives in another state, so I could not drop it by her house. She asked me to mail it to her, so I did. When I check my credit card purchases, I see the charge for postage. Where does this fit in my budget? I do not have a category called postage or reimbursement, but I have a miscellaneous category. I usually do not remember to collect these small amounts from my kids, so maybe I could put it into the category called gifts? Hmmm

The problem can arise when we have too many small, unusual purchases. At that point, you need to analyze these to see if they should fit somewhere else or if you need to group some of them into a new category. Use the notes section for your purchases so you have an idea what and why you purchased this item.

Below is a suggestion for a simple budget. This is a SUGGESTION. It may or may not work for you, but it can be a beginning point.

Housing (25%-40%)

- Rent or mortgage
- Utilities (can include electric/gas, internet, phone, water/sewer, trash)
- Maintenance (repairs, yard work, small projects)

Food (10%-15%)

- Groceries (all items regularly bought at a grocery store)
- Restaurants (all eating out and take out occasions)

Transportation (10%-15%)

- Car payment
- Insurance
- Gas/tolls
- Maintenance
- Note: Some people may need line item for taxis/Uber/subways

Medical (10%-20%)

- Insurance
- Deductibles/Copays
- Note: do not forget to include dental and eye care

Clothing (5%)

Giving (5%-15%)

- Special Occasions (Birthday/anniversary/get well...)
- Christmas
- Donations (churches or other non-profits)

Entertainment (5%-10%)

- Memberships/Subscriptions
- Special outings (tickets to a game, going to a movie...)
- Hobbies

Miscellaneous (beware of the black hole!) (1%-2%)

Savings (10%-15%)

- Emergency fund
- Retirement/Investments
- Vacations
- My dream items... (new car, travel, house down payment...)

I excluded business since this should be kept separate from your personal budget.

You will notice next to each main category is a percentage amount. This amount is more like a guide. Each person's budget will be different. If you are way off on one category and it matches your values, then it is OK. We each have various goals, so it comes to reason that our percentages will be different.

If you added up all the higher percentages, you would come up with 137%. If you add up all the lower percentages, you will come up with 81%. Your goal is to hit 100% of your income; therefore, you will be closer to the higher percentage on some and the lower scale on others. Each person's budget is unique.

Also, note that business does not have a percentage since these are write-off expenses and should not be included in your personal budget. Business and personal should always remain separate. You may have a percentage of your income that goes into your business, but this is an investment, not a part of your personal living expenses.

Besides having diverse values and goals, we are also different in our stages of life. A young couple who just bought a house may have a higher percentage in the housing category than most people. Another couple whose kids have all moved out may have more money going into retirement than most of us. Someone else may have a high value of exploration, so they have a large amount in a category called travel.

What is listed above is just an idea. The wonderful thing about budgets is that you create something that fits you. You can name them whatever you want. You can put in whatever percentage or amount you feel you need to in each group so you can attain your own personal goals.

There are a couple of rules you need to follow.:

- Plan for the future
- Only budget your expenses based on your income

* * *

Assignment:

1. Take your expense list and add an extra column. This column will be your sub or minor category list.
2. Write the subcategory that fits best next to each expense .

Expenses Sub-Category Sample

Date	Vendor	Description	Amount	Major Category	Sub-Category
June 15	Food King	groceries	112.58	Food	Grocceries
June 5	Pub Master	friends eating out	29.00	Food	Resturant
June 22	Big Mart	Jackie's birthday	21.42	Giving	Special Occasions
June 10	AC Power	electric	119.00	Housing	Utilities
June 22	WWW Connect	internet	83.08	Housing	Utilities
July 1	WWW Connect	internet	83.08	Housing	Utilities
June 16	GoGoGas	gas	39.42	Transportation	Gas/Tolls

19

Exercise Break

My wife has run marathons and ended up talking me into running. I could not picture myself running for hours so I agreed to run a half-marathon as long as it was a trail run. At least I could look at the beautiful landscape as I ran through the woods. During my time of training, people would frequently asked if I loved running. I did not. I ran because it was good for me and it was something I occasionally did with my wife. Running is not pleasurable to me, but now I can say I ran a half marathon and there is a bit of pride when I tell people I run.

You may feel the same about budgeting as I do running. You may not enjoy the process but in the end you will feel better and be able to tell people that you have mastered this thing called personal finances. Now is the time we will perform an exercise with your new skills of budgeting.

You will need either a pencil/paper or, if you like, you can do this on a spreadsheet like Excel or Google docs. Gather the list you made of all your income and expenses over the last 3 to 6 months. If you do not have bank statements or credit card bills, your memory will have to suffice.

Creative Idea: You can download your bank and credit card statements into a spreadsheet and sort them by description, vendor, and date. In this way, you can easily calculate averages spent in a month for a particular item.

If we are budgeting with a purpose, let's make categories that fit that purpose. On the top of a page, write out the first major category. We can start with the biggest – housing. Next, you can begin listing expenses that have something to do with the place where you live. When you list these expenses, put in the date, the amount, and who you paid. You may also need to put in what the purchase was. If you already have subcategories, you can add those as well.

Housing Example:

June 2: $83.08 – WWW Connection - internet/cable
June 10: $119.00 – AC Power - electric
June 17: $792.00 – Sweet Home Reality – rent
June 21: $59.42 – Home Depot – paint supplies for bedroom
July 2: $80.40 – WWW Connection - internet/cable
July 8: $131.00 – AC Power
July 17: $792.00 – Sweet Home Reality – rent

Remember to look for non-monthly expenses like water/sewer or seasonal costs like oil to heat the furnace in the winter.

May 5: $68.12 – Fountain County – water/sewer (bi-monthly)
July 6: $76.55 – Fountain County – water/sewer (bi-monthly)
January 18: $352.00 – Hot Head Oil – furnace fuel (yearly)

Items that are the same every month are easy to budget. For our example, rent is $792.00 every month. When I look at electricity or water/sewer, these fluctuate. Then we have heating oil that may only happens once a year. I like grouping these into one category versus many because I only have to manage one number. I can budget an average, so when one is high, maybe the other is low. Averages spread over several similar items are simple to predict rather than having to focus on each one individually. I strongly suggest to round up high to protect yourself from inflation and unexpected changes.

Here is what I would have for our monthly budget example:

Housing

Rent = **$792.00**

Utilities = **$275.00** (rounded up from actual average)

-Electricity (119+131 / 2 months) = $125.00

-Water/Sewer (68.12+76.55 / 4 months) = $36.17

-Heating oil (352 / 12 months usage) = $29.33

-Internet/Cable (83.08+80.40 / 2 months) = $81.74

-Total average = $272.24

Improvements = **$50.00**

Total Housing = **$1,117.00**

Note: since I rent, the landlord takes care of the maintenance, but I prefer to make my house a home, like painting, adding plants, etc. - I created an improvements category and budgeted some fun money to do this.

Caution:

With any budget, you are doing your best to predict the future. Inflation, life changes, and unexpected expenses must be considered and added. Stress is avoided when you plan for unforeseen repairs and emergencies.

I recently took my car in for a routine inspection and oil change. The car was five years old, and the mileage was almost 40,000. It ran fine, so I was not expecting any real issues. I thought I might have another year on the tires, but they did not pass inspection. There were a few other small things, and the bill was over $800.00. I had a category called car maintenance, and I had budgeted $150 a month, so I had enough money to cover this. I was not stressed because history has taught me that my cars will need regular maintenance and usually one big bill a year. When you expect the unexpected and even plan for it, you are not surprised, you have the money to cover it, and best of all, you do not even have to think about it. Planning reduces stress.

In my example, I used just a couple of months. The more data you have over a longer period will help you predict the future more accurately. Glancing over the past 12 months should be fine for most of us.

Your goal now is to take this exercise and develop it into all your categories and subcategories. Your budget is now evolving into something that will help you plan for your future.

* * *

Assignment:

Your list of expenses should already be sorted in this order:

1. Major category
2. Subcategory
3. Vendor
4. Date

You should have several months of data listed. Now we can find out what you are spending per category.

- Like we did for housing earlier in this chapter, average out the monthly expenses per subcategory.
- Give each major category a total by adding up all of it's subcategories.

20

Puzzle Pieces

A few years ago I gave my son one of those 3D puzzles. It was a movie projector that worked. When we were building it, the pieces were not staying together very well, so we decided to add glue to secure certain connections. After putting it back together, we still had a few leftover parts. The projector may work without them, but we agreed that we should go back to the instructions and find out where these parts go and do it right.

Your budget may look complete, but it is still missing a few parts. We have a few more steps for it to work correctly, so hang in there.

The first missing part is comparing your income to your expenses. Hopefully, the gap is not too large. If your expenses exceed your income, you need to reevaluate how you allocate your income. This is typically my issue. Cutting expenses can be challenging. Looking over those items like food, entertainment, clothing, and miscellaneous is an excellent place to start.

The hard decisions become more manageable when you have the right motivation. I heard of two brothers who lived in a tent in the woods, took cold showers under a waterfall, and ate hot dogs and Ramen noodles so they could save up money to buy a car. To save money for a trip, another young man turned off the oil furnace, took hot showers twice a day, and wore his heavy coat inside to stay warm. I do not recommend these somewhat extreme actions, but I think you get the point.

For an easier way, maybe get a part-time job or even change careers. I do not know your circumstances, but you do. And you know that you are not happy with things right now, so changes need to be made. You have a different vision for life, so ask for help, get counsel, make a plan, and follow through.

Once you have made these hard decisions and your expenses equal your income, you need to map out how each paycheck will be allocated. If you get paid twice a month, then make a decision now on where this money will go. Each paycheck has a purpose. Deciding before you have the money will make it easier than after you have the money. If you do not plan it, the money will disappear. It is the same with bonus money, overtime pay, and tax refunds. You have to plan it out while your head is clear, and the temptation to spend it on whatever catches your eye is low.

This may be the point when reality kicks in. Our needs plus our wants far exceeds our ability to pay for them. You have a couple of choices. The first is to act like an ostrich. When difficult times come, he just puts his head in the sand hoping it will all go away. Problems just don't go away; they usually produce new ones. Giving up and continually living your life the same old way does not work. Hopefully you caught enough of what I have been saying to not be satisfied with where you are and to realize you do not want to live with regret. This brings us to the best option: moving forward. You are smarter than you think. You have talents that will take you to the next step. You are responsible enough to own your future.

* * *

Assignment:

Let's take a moment and recap what you are doing.

1. Calculate your monthly income (do not count bonuses and gifts)
2. Gather your expenses (monthly, non-monthly, annual)
3. Come up with general categories
4. Put your expenses in each of your general categories
5. Create specific categories and label on your expenses
6. Calculate a monthly average for each specific category
7. Compare income to expenses *(new)*
8. Cut what needs to be cut *(new)*
9. Map out where you will allocate each paycheck to cover specific expenses *(new)*

Most of what we have done so far reveals our historical spending patterns. If you did not have a budget or just recorded spending not to exceed income, then your money has not taken you very far. For years, I have always had a budget, but my budget was designed to keep me out of debt. Whatever money came in was budgeted to go out. If I made more, I could spend more. I failed to realize a budget is more than a record of the past. It needs to be a plan for the future. What I had failed to do, is what you need to do next.

21

Onward We Go...

A couple of months ago, my son had to be at a function early in the morning, and I needed to drive him. I am an early riser, so I was up and ready to take him. I believe he had a late night, so he was moving a little slow that morning. He just could not get out of first gear. The good dad that I am, I decided to help him by making him an on-the-go breakfast. I looked around the kitchen and found a bagel. I had time, so I toasted it and spread some cream cheese on the top of each half. He came downstairs just in time to leave. He thanked me for the bagel, and off we went. As we pulled out of the driveway, I noticed that his expression changed when he took a bite of the bagel. His face looked slightly contorted, and the bagel was now coming out of his mouth instead of going in. He asked me what I put on the bagel. I said cream cheese. He said it was not cream cheese. It was sour cream. Ooops! The containers looked the same. Each had the word cream in the name. The contents were both white, but the taste was vastly different.

My son managed to eat a couple of bites to reduce his hunger, but it was not very satisfying. Your budget may feel the same way right now. It looks good, works, and helps you manage your money, but something does not taste right. You need to replace the sour cream with cream cheese. Your budget needs to change the focus from controlling spending to realizing your vision. You need to do more than manage your money. You need to direct it towards where you want to go, aligning it with your vision.

There were things we laid out earlier in the book that should help you direct your life in a specific direction. This is the place where hard decisions are made, but these decisions will affect the rest of your life. You need to take your values and create specific categories or action items for each one of them.

Let's look at a few examples:

I have a friend who values space and the peaceful feel of a small community. The problem is he works in New York. He moved his family to a small town over an hour and a half away. He commutes to and from work every day. He gets a lot of work done on the train. They value scenic serenity.

There was a couple that valued travel. While all their friends were buying big homes in the suburbs, they decided to purchase a small condo where they could bike and walk to work. The money they saved from lower mortgage payments and maintaining only one car went to big vacations overseas. They valued adventure.

One young man values healthy living, so he has a gym membership. He also spends more on groceries since healthy foods tend to cost more. He sacrifices eating out and limits his entertainment budget to pay for these things he values.

You may find that some goals need to be set aside because you do not have the resources and time to attain all of them. Someone who plans to buy a house and also dreams of traveling the country with his accordion in a rock and roll band may not be able to reach both goals at the same time unless he has a successful recording contract. Most bands are lucky to break even when they travel to small venues, and the members also need to take off work to perform. Both are dreams and fantastic goals, but one costs resources, and the other requires a lot of resources to be saved up.

When I was younger, I thought about being a photographer and traveling the world for National Geographic. I realized very early that I was not that good of a photographer and that this skill should be more of a hobby than a profession. Some dreams are made to be hobbies, and other dreams end up being replaced by better ones.

When you get married, things can shift. When you have children, everything changes. With these changes come new values, and new dreams. We should not think we are giving up on old dreams; instead, we are replacing them with better ones. It is OK. This is life. We all change and grow. Do not live in the past; live in the now and prepare for the future.

Whatever your values are, you need a plan to reach them. You need to budget for them and make sacrifices in other areas. When you achieve your goals, there is a sense of satisfaction and accomplishment.

How you move your plan forward requires vision. Now is the time to create a plan that includes those dreams. Very rarely do things just fall in your lap. Few of us will win the lottery or inherit a million dollars from some unknown uncle. It takes one step at a time and may take years to come. In the end, it will be worth it.

Your values require sacrifice. Sacrifice can take on many forms. Cutting back on spending so you can save is just one of those. Education is another. You need to become an expert in what you dream about. If you like to travel, plan a trip; review how others have done it; read books about where you are going. If you like biking, find out about all the types of bikes available and how to repair them. You can also get a part-time job with a company related to your dream. You can learn and gain extra cash to support where you want to go.

The HOW we have been talking about is the plan to make your values real. The plan includes a budget. Do not just talk about it. Step beyond your fear and take action. Journeys begin when you put one foot in front of the other. Take your first step forward.

Make that budget.

V

WHEN

The bad news is time flies. The good news is you're the pilot.

Michael Altshuler

22

What is Truth?

When will you decide what is true? The truth you believe is the truth that will move you to take the next step. The truth is, no matter how bad it may look, you can overcome the things that prevent you from making a budget. Like any plan, it requires thought, study, discipline, and vision. The truth is it will not happen overnight. It takes time. It takes you deciding that you will take one step and then one more step.

A few years ago, I went to the doctor for an annual physical. It had been some time since I had my last visit, and I knew that the busyness of life had affected my health. The doctor did the routine physical with weight, height, blood pressure reading, and labs. A couple of weeks later, I had a follow-up visit and was told my cholesterol was high. The doctor wanted to prescribe me medication. To be honest, I was a little concerned. A few years earlier, my dad had a stroke and could no longer do the things he enjoyed. This was hard on my mother since she had to care for him. I did not want this to happen to me or my family. I have never been a fan of becoming dependent on medications. So, I asked my doctor if there was an alternative. He told me to start exercising, eat better, and lose weight. In a few months, we agreed to take another look at my labs.

I quickly realized that gaining weight is easier than losing it. I joined the YMCA, intending to work out three to four times a week. I tried to go after work, but sometimes it was not feasible. I had to move my routine to early mornings. It was hard to get my body going. Waking up early and relaxing with a cup of coffee is one thing. Getting up early to make my body work hard is another. After a while, my workouts became a new routine that was easier physically and mentally. MY weight-loss goal included changing my eating habits. Not having ice cream every evening was a discipline. I researched various diets and decided to cut out a lot of my sugars and carbs. I worked hard, and within a few months, I was almost back to my pre-marriage weight. The next doctor visit revealed cholesterol levels that were back in an acceptable range—no pills for me.

My point is this; like dieting, budgets take work that requires daily decisions. The truth is a whole lot of small decisions over time can make a significant impact on your life. It is like brushing your teeth for two to three minutes twice a day. While brushing your teeth once does not significantly affect the health of your teeth, doing this daily will produce a healthy mouth. Similarly, daily spending decisions will also affect the health of your bank account. You get to choose.

Making small decisions would not be so hard if it were not for obstacles. The truth is obstacles are a part of life. They are not a possibility; they are a guarantee. We do our best to plan for them, but we do not have a crystal ball telling us what is around the next corner. Obstacles do have a purpose. They make us stronger. They build mental stamina. They teach us patience. We experience success with each obstacle we overcome. This breeds confidence and increases our ability to overcome greater obstacles. We have a life more satisfying, our joys become richer, and our relationships become deeper. Our compassion for others who are struggling grows and inspires us to lend a helping hand. If we allow them, obstacles can make us into better people.

Sometimes we fail; we make mistakes. Welcome to the human race. Just like obstacles, failures are a part of life. On April 8, 1974, Hank Aaron broke Babe Ruth's long time home run record and later ended his career with 755 home runs. He holds the major league records for most all star games, extra base hits, runs batted in, and total bases. By the way, he also had 1,383 strikeouts, hundreds of fly balls, and numerous times being thrown out at first base. In fact, 70% of the time he went to bat, he did not even get on base. The point was to keep getting up to bat. In his career, Hank went to bat 12,364 times.[21] He had many, many swings. His failures did not prevent him from swinging. Without his "keep swinging" mindset he would never had broken the home run record.

I used to play a little golf. By a little, I mean three to four times a year. I am usually competitive in sports or games, but I realized that golf was a game of extremes. I could make a great shot and follow it by shanking the ball into the woods. I soon learned to relax and enjoy time with friends rather than stressing over my last poor attempt. My goal changed from producing a low score to coming home with more golf balls than I started with. Every time my shot went off in the woods, I would finding extra golf balls that others had lost. The truth is sometimes your goals need to be changed, and you learn to find better ones.

I tell you these things to let you know that failures are common. This is how we learn. The goal here is not to have losses, but to learn from them, and to make adjustments that move us closer to our goals.

---

[21] https://www.baseball-almanac.com/players/player.php?p=aaronha01

My son ran cross-country. Running is different than most team sports. When I was a kid, I played football. I remember how the coach emphasized that each player had a role, and every position was critical to success. In cross country, only the top six runners' time counts. At first, I wondered why there were fifteen or so players on the team. If only the first six impacted the result, what was the purpose of the other runners? Why were they running? When I went to a meet, I noticed that after the best runners finished their race, they would return to the finish line and cheer on the rest of their teammates. They stayed there until the last member of their team finished the race, cheering them on till their voices were horse. High fives, hugs, and congratulations were abounding. The secret I missed is that the players were not running against each other as much as they were competing against themselves. They were always trying to get a PR – a personal record. Their goal was to improve themselves.

Another truth you must realize is that life is not a competition against those around you. Stop comparing yourself to others. It is easy to see people's successes but harder to see their failures. On the outside, they may look great, but things could be falling apart on the inside. The goal is not to keep up with the Jones'. The goal is to be the best you that you can be. Like a runner, your focus is on improving yourself.

When we take our eyes off others, things inside us change. We tend to stop blaming others for our problems. We no longer look for others to bail us out. Our desire to look better than our friends and acquaintances drifts away. We tend to value personal integrity instead of hiding who we are.

Working a budget is one step toward being your best self. Your focus is on what you have and how you are responsible for it. Money becomes more than something you wish you had more of and becomes something that can be used to provide for your needs and affect the world around you. Is that not something we all long for? We desire to find our place in this world and how we can positively impact those we love.

The truth is a budget is not a guarantee of success; it is a piece of the puzzle. It is a plan to move us toward success. Remember, a failure to plan is a plan to fail. If we do not make a budget, we have already lost. It is time to take those small steps that move you forward and overcome those obstacles. You can do this. Your budget allows you to move forward to accomplish your vision for your life, one day at a time.

And that is the truth.

23

Budgeting Tools

In June 2021, The Penny Hoarder reported that 40% of people who budget use a spreadsheet to track their finances.[22] On the other hand, I would recommend you use an online program. These applications have already done the demanding work to make managing your money simpler. My goal is to manage my money, not recreate the wheel repeatedly. Most cost money, but a worker is worth his hire, so go ahead and pay them. It is worth it.

This last section is a review of several online budgeting tools that are available to us. I have used many of these, and some I have just looked over. Various reviews and opinions from others have been combined with my own to try to give you a balanced review. Different programs fit different people. The best one for you will probably have to do more with preference than anything else. Most of these programs have a 30-day free trial but resist the temptation of switching too often because you will get burned out and confused. Remember, what you read is an opinion.

---

[22] https://www.thepennyhoarder.com/budgeting/budgeting-statistics/

Questions to ask when reviewing a budget app:

1. How easy is it to learn, and is it visually appealing? (If it is too difficult to understand, I will give up)
2. Do you want to manually enter transactions, or have it sync to your bank/credit card/investment accounts?
3. Can you customize your categories and delete unused ones?
4. Does it automatically categorize new transactions for you, or do you do this yourself? (I strongly suggest you do this yourself – suggestions are OK but not complete automation)
5. Can I split transactions between categories?
6. How does it distinguish new transactions from old ones? (This allows me to know what I need to work on)
7. Does it give you notifications? (Bills due/overspending)
8. Do notifications disappear, or do I need to fix them before they go away?
9. Does it allow me to roll over my excess in a category to the next month's spending plan?
10. How easy is it to make changes, move money between categories, or move subcategories to different main categories?
11. Can you set up income to automatically allocate to each spending category? (Automation for income is preferred but manual is OK – If I make the same amount every paycheck, I do not want to have to keep recreating the wheel)
12. Does the program have training and good customer support?
13. Can I download transactions into a spreadsheet?
14. How far back does it upload my history of transactions when I first start?
15. How in-depth is the reporting? Can I compare expenses from one month to another / can I run by vendor or notes / etc?
16. What is the monthly/annual cost?

MINT - https://mint.intuit.com/

By far, Mint has the most significant share of the market. The last figure I found was about twenty-five million users. Its biggest draw is that it is free. The company makes its money by posting ads on its program. When I used Mint, the ads did not bother me too much, but for others, it was annoying. The program also does a decent job of looking at your total financial picture, like savings, home ownership, and retirement.

Philosophy:

- When I review Mint, I see a basic program designed to look at all aspects of your financials.

Advantages:

- All your accounts in one place – Checking/Savings/Credit Cards/Loans/Retirement/Credit Score
- It's free! (I like free)
- You can set up alarms for bill pay, low balances, and overspending – but these are easy to ignore
- Account automatically links up, so there is no manual entering of transactions
- All expense categories are already set up for you
- You can create your own new categories

Disadvantage:

- Their standard categories cannot be deleted (way too many....)
- It automatically assigns expenses to a category, and it is hard to tell new purchases from old ones that you have already reviewed – (confusing)

- There is not a lot of guidance for new budgeters on how to budget effectively
- I found the reporting aspect subpar (like comparing expenses month to month)
- Money not spent in an expense category does not roll over to the next month (you can turn this feature on, but it messes up reporting)
- It tends to lead people to a hands-off approach due to its automation of expense categories

Best for:

- Those who want all their finances in one place and those who have control over their spending

Summary:

I found Mint to be overly automated. My goal is to manage my own money, not have someone else do it. I had a challenging time getting the specific reports I needed so I could manage my money. Mint was a good program for someone to record their spending, not necessarily manage their money.

YNAB - https://www.youneedabudget.com/

People who love budgeting love YNAB. They have a cult-like following. I tried YNAB for a month, and I thought it was an excellent program, just not for me. Their approach is different than most. You can only budget the money you have in the bank, not the money you plan on getting. This does make it a little confusing when you try to plan ahead, but it is a great way to help people limit their spending. They boast that the average new budgeter saves over $600 in the first two months and $6,000 in their first year.

Philosophy:

- Every dollar has a job, and you can only budget what you have in the bank. This is an electronic version of the envelope method.

Advantages:

- They have excellent teaching videos to help you understand their ideas on handling your money.
- They encourage flexibility, like moving money from one category to the other when you overspend – emphases are on giving yourself the grace to make mistakes.
- They use the term Age Your Money. This means that when this month's expenses are budgeted, you use any excess funds to budget next month's expenses. It is another word for savings, but they use it to cover future month's expenses.
- One of the best for behavioral change
- Flexibility with categories
- A lot of support in the YNAB community
- Excess money for a category rolls over to the next month.
- Notifications require action
- New transactions are separate from old ones, with suggested categories based on the last use

Disadvantage:

- There is a learning curve since their philosophy on budgeting only what you have does not follow traditional income forecasting
- The current price is $14.99 a month or $98.99 a year ($8.25/month)
- No bill payment alerts
- They do not track investments, credit scores, or retirement planning

- Cannot automate income into categories
- No budgeting forecasting (it does not populate the amount needed for budgeting; you must use the goals setting)
- Delay in credit card transactions hitting budget

Best for:

- Those who need help controlling their spending. Great for behavioral changes.

Summary:
YNAB is a great program. The mind switch was a little too much for me, and I found the forward planning a little confusing. It is also a little expensive for my taste.

Good introductory video:

- Lara Hammock Pros and Cons from a Former Mint User - https://www.youtube.com/watch?v=z3kpRrOluTo

EveryDollar – https://www.ramseysolutions.com/ramseyplus/everydollar

This is the Dave Ramsey plan based on zero-based budgeting. Like YNAB, every dollar has a job. It also is designed to pay yourself first, which means saving before spending. This budget program has over a million users and has both a free and paid version. The free vision has the same basic features as the paid but lacks some of the nice features like syncing to your bank accounts, being about to download your transaction to a spreadsheet, and receiving tracking reminders. The paid version also gives you access to Dave Ramsey's financial peace university materials which is well worth watching.

Philosophy:

- Every dollar is given a purpose (zero-based budgeting), emphasizing getting out of debt and helping you focus on your goals. It is based on Dave Ramsey's seven baby steps to financial freedom.

Advantages:

- Very clear with an easy-to-use workflow – strong visual aesthetics
- Set up takes you through your financial goals
- Customize your categories
- Access to financial education programs (paid version)
- Automated expenses tracking (paid version)
- Split transactions
- Set bill due dates
- Follows Dave Ramsey's Baby Steps program

Disadvantage:

- Price - $59.99 for 3 month ($20/month)$99.99 for 6 months ($16.66/month),or $129.99 per year ($10.83/month)– unless you pay for a year's subscription the price is high
- No credit monitoring
- No investment tracking
- Subcategories cannot be moved to be under a different major category
- For expense accounts, money not spent one month does not roll over to the next month. Note: categories can be set up as funds that do create a rollover effect

- The free version continually prompts you to join the paid version
- Does not anticipate vendors or categories from previous uses
- Does not keep bank account amounts so you can reconcile
- Does not hold you accountable for overspending
- Reporting is minimal
- Using credit cards for everyday purchases and then paying them off requires extra steps.

Best for:

People who are trying to get out of debt and need a simple budget. It is also great for goal setting.

Summary:

There is a wealth of information and educational material. The free version is too manual for me, and the premium version is too expensive. The training material is great, but I do not think I would need them any longer after a year. The simplicity of the program is attractive.

Good introductory video:

- Morgan Stradling, How To Use EveryDollar App https://www.youtube.com/watch?v=8KVSu-DbixQ

Tiller Money – https://www.tillerhq.com

Tiller is a great program that fits well for people who love spreadsheets. They have complimentary reviews for ease of use and customer support. Their program can be set up to automatically download transactions from your financial institutions, and they also have pre-built templates to get you going. You can customize about everything so it will fit you.

Philosophy:

- A very hands-on and customizable platform that uses spreadsheets.

Advantages:

- Customize everything – flexible, even customize transactions to pick a category automatically
- Auto update with banking/credit cards
- 30-day free trial
- You can create multiple budgets for personal, business, or spouse
- Only you see your data – not even Tiller has access to it
- Works with Excel or Google sheets
- Big community for support

Disadvantages:

- No mobile app – but you can use Glide to create one[21]
- No credit score, bill management, or retirement planning
- Cost $79/ Year ($6.58/month), not really a negative
- Not suitable for people who are intimidated by spreadsheets
- I found it a little confusing to set up, so there is a learning curve

Best For:

- People who understand spreadsheets and like to customize everything.

---

[23] https://www.glideapps.com/blog/make-your-own-tiller-money-app-with-glide

Summary:
Tiller is highly flexible. The downside to having so many options is difficulty. Unless you understand spreadsheets, this is not for you. This is not for beginner-budgeters. It is powerful, and the price is reasonable.

Good introductory video:

- Heather with Tiller: How to use the Tiller Foundation Template - https://www.youtube.com/watch?v=yNb0k42_XUo

There are many more programs out there. Here is a quick look at a few more ...

- Simplify: created by Quicken – far too much automation, cannot customize, but low cost and simple.
- Mvelopes: a good program but too glitchy. I used this one for years, but when they made an updated version, changes were difficult, and I no longer trusted what they were doing.
- Personal Capital: Great for looking at your total net worth but a deficient budget program.
- CountAbout: Great for downloading previous transactions from Mint and Quicken. It has options for small business, like invoicing and adding copies of receipts; 45-day trial; download transactions, flexible categories
- PocketGuard: A complete automated budgeting app with spending reports and estimated goal tracking. It has a unique feature that divides your estimated income and bills to produce an amount that is "in your pocket" which is your safe amount you can spend on anything. My thoughts, this is way to automated if you want to manage your own money.

- Honeydue: A budget app designed for you and your partner. Note,there is no desktop feature, just a phone app. They have three sections: one for you, one for your partner, and one to share. You can even communicate with your partner through the app. It is free but has advertisements. The app is limited, and the support is not great.

Concluding thoughts:

Budgets are personal, and no program will be perfect. I suggest you take the plunge and stick with a program for one year before making changes. Developing a good rhythm and habits that affect your financial freedom usually takes a year.

24

Conclusion

As I write this book, I am reminded that we live in a time of uncertainty. As my son texted me the other day, “We are currently seeing record highs in inflation and corporate profits, while also seeing skyrocketing rents, the housing market, and groceries. It’s hard for people to make ends meet now than ever, and/or save for their dreams.” I agree with my son and his evaluation of our country’s current situation. The question is, what do we do with this information? We can let the current landscape deter us, or we can search for ways to move forward. The important thing is that we do not give up hope.

I hope you realized that this book on budgeting is more than dealing with money. It is about dreams and finding the tools needed to make them a reality. Finding the right tools are important, but it is the dreams that keep you going.

Let me tell you about a man named Walter. He was born in Chicago and was the fourth of five children. His family moved a few times as his dad would try to find w ork. There were several business adventures that his father started, but most of them met with tragedy. He quit school after eighth grade and started working odd jobs. He was not very good at business and even owed one employer money at the end of the summer due to his incompetence.

Walter loved to draw and submitted cartoons to humor magazines but was often rejected. He landed his first big job at a commercial art studio but was laid off after the first month. The next job he had was in multi-media. He soon saw the advantages that were in this industry, so he started his own company. He was so nervous when he presented his product to his first client that when he was asked the price, he quoted his cost. He ended up doing several projects with zero profit. Within a few years the company went bankrupt.

His next company had a few successes, but he dreamed of something more. There was one project that he embarked on that his critics called the folly that would destroy him. Even his family tried to talk him out of it, but he pushed forward. His company was running out of money and after several tries, he finally secured the finances to stay afloat.

When his special project was finally completed it became a huge success, producing a return of $8 million. This was in 1938 which would be about $134 million in today's money. The project was called *Snow White and the Seven Dwarfs*.[24]

---

[24] https://www.learningliftoff.com/overcoming-obstacles-hard-work-and-persistence-paid-off-for-walt-disney/

If you had not guessed, I have been talking about Walt Disney. He lived through the great depression, World War I and World War II. He worked on a farm, as a paperboy, in concession sales, as an ambulance driver, and finally an artist. He developed a vision that was bigger than himself. He employed others to help sure up the areas where he lacked. Even though he lived during depressive times, wars, and saw many personal setbacks, he kept moving forward. He never took his eye off the goal. He never stopped dreaming. May we live our dreams with the same optimism and fortitude.

It seems best to end Budgeting Without Money with a quote from Walt Disney,

"All our dreams can come true,
if we have the courage to pursue them." [25]

[25] https://parade.com/1120968/alexandra-hurtado/walt-disney-quotes/ge

My Budget

	Month		
	Budget	Actual	Difference
Housing			
Rent			
Utilities			
Maintenance			
Food			
Groceries			
Eating Out			
Transportation			
Car payment			
Insurance			
Gas/tolls			
Maintenance			
Medical			
Insurance			
Deductible/Copay			
Clothing			
Clothing			
Giving			
Special Occasions			
Christmas			
Donations			
Entertainment			
Memberships			
Special outings			
Hobbies			
Miscellaneous			
Miscellaneous			
Savings			
Emergency fund			
Retirement			
Vacations			
My dream items			
Monthly Totals			
Totals			

Made in the USA
Monee, IL
04 November 2026

67377451R00085